**08** Steps to Be in the Zone

The Mathematics, Metaphysics and Magic of 108

By Ethan Indigo Smith

~Dedicated to all nurses, healers and homeopaths of the world.

Contents

Introduction to Energy

Do not just go with the flow, flow with the flow.

The above image is of an energized person radiating a Merkaba, symbolizing balance and the power of self. The word Merkaba has ancient Egyptian etymological roots combining 3 concepts, Mer means counter rotating fields of light, Ka means spirit and Ba means body. In Hebrew Merkaba has come to mean chariot or vehicle. The counter rotational fields of light of the Merkaba symbolize balancing the physical and spiritual, and the feminine with the masculine, so as to properly energize our personal consciousness vehicles.

The 24 sided, 8 pointed Merkaba or stellated octahedron is made up of two tetrahedrons (four sided pyramids) spinning in harmonious opposition. It is mathematically significant as one of the 5 Platonic Solids, designs which hold deep mathematical and metaphysical insights. The Merkaba represents the element fire. The other Platonic Solids represent the other theorized elements of air, water, earth and ethereal.

The Merkaba is biblically related to the vision of Ezekiel in which he sees a divine wheel or chariot, the Merkaba, and sets of four wheels and four heads in relation to it. Ezekiel's vision is often referred to as an allegory for meditative connection with the elemental energies. Many meditations from diverse practices have ideas within them pertaining to the idea of counter rotational spirit/body energy. Among every tradition I am aware of, the left side of the body is feminine, the right side is masculine, while our feet are grounded to the feminine earth body and the crown of our head is attached to the masculine spirit energy above. Imagining the counter rotational mixing of feminine/masculine and sprit/body energies symbolically depicted in the Merkaba is one of the first important steps in numerous meditations. The synergy of such balance leads to quality energy, enhanced abilities including increased capability for metaphysical awareness.

Many have sought to experience the visionary energy like Ezekiel, while others have tried to suppress interest in the energy represented by the counter rotational Merkaba and depicted in the Vision of Ezekiel by maintaining meditative energy is negative in some way or that intangible energy is somehow a crock. The energy in Ezekiel's vision is likely the same energy described in chi gung, tai chi and yoga. In fact the Merkaba can be seen as having many of the same attributes as the Yin Yang if one simply imagines the Yin Yang as a three dimensional form. The main reason for perpetuated stigmatized labels on meditation and meditative energy to the point of fear and mockery is because some do not want others to access the energy for their individuation. They prefer others do not study meditation and do not enhance themselves with potentially visionary energy. Worldlings, the fools and the fooling, would have you believe there is only the tangible and mechanical, but metaphysical energy and invisible insight are intangible and cannot be held, but real nonetheless.

Many people were not allowed to publicly read and were all out prevented from studying the Ezekiel text in the past, likely because of the meditative powers the text hinted at and authorities that wanted to restrict access to understanding it. The biblical text of Ezekiel was variously restricted over time, just like other meditation teachings with various origins were hidden and restricted. Meditation and meditative movements like tai chi, chi gung and yoga all have similarly secretive pasts and aspects.

Information on meditative movement has practically always been restricted and hidden, partly because if meditative movement is done with an improper state of mind it can be harmful to the practitioner. But the main reason for information restriction is people with an improper mind state tend to harm and take from others. There have always been those with improper mind states who withhold information to maintain power over others. And alternatively there have always been those who withheld information to prevent those with improper mind states from obtaining more knowledge for more power over others. The main reason for secrets of any sort is to gain and maintain power though. The main symbol of Freemasonry, considered to be a highly secretive group, is the (feminine) compass and the (masculine) square symbolizing the Merkaba with two pillars or lines missing. This can represent and correlate with the Merkaba, only with aspects withheld.

The Merkaba illustrates, through exoteric and esoteric symbolism, balanced interaction of positive and negative fields, of masculine and feminine, of heavenly and earthly energy rotating in harmonious opposition. Movement in harmonious opposition results in quality energy exemplified in electrical current. And just as electrical energy is not imaginary, but we often cannot see it, individual energy is the same, real and mostly unseen. And in the same way that electrical energy requires positive and negative flows our individual energy requires such harmonious opposition too, just as represented by the Merkaba.

The downward facing tetrahedron or pyramid revolves from right to left and represents the feminine or negative aspect. The upward facing tetrahedron revolves from left to right and represents the masculine or positive aspect. The word pyramid is made up of two words. Pyr means fire and amid means in the middle. The inferred concept is fire in the middle. And in the middle of the Merkaba is the midline holding it all together. The Merkaba represents energy, chi, prana, the electromagnetic field and/or the spark of god permeating into and emitting from everything. And the more balanced a being or consciousness vehicle is, the more one walks the mid line or middle path, the more fire and quality energy becomes available to help ourselves and others.

The Merkaba is a metaphysical representation of balanced energy through the combination of geometrical importance and biblical reference, in its Egyptian etymological origins and Old Testament usage. Metaphysical ideas, like the Merkaba, contain scientific and theological correlation as well as ideas applicable to stimulate the mind and spirit.

We have yet to completely understand the spark of electricity and electromagnetics entirely and yet we use electromagnetic current every day in buildings and machines. In the same way we mostly have yet to totally understand the universal creative life force of chi, prana, entheos, orgone, the fire within resulting in our own individual energy, but we use it too.

Once you give an electromagnetic current a counterbalanced outlet, it powers up and releases. Chi, prana, the universal life force works in the same way, once you consciously focus balanced connection the energy powers the outlet, the outlet being you. And as machines take time to build our connection requires building too. Strengthening the connection within ourselves, finding our way to our own Zone is a process, like writing a book. One can only write a page or two a day. But eventually you have a book which can teach and is layered as thin frail papers forming together a binder which cannot be torn.

Energy is energy, the life force or consciousness is the same. Whether it's a plant, or a planet, or a person everything has an electromagnetic field giving off and receiving energy, depending on the being or vehicle, different forms of energy are presented and received. To be a better transformer of energy it is necessary to develop self and this can often only be done through a process, as if writing, one page at a time.

The Merkaba is a geometrical representation of the natural or biological formation called a torus. A torus is an energy field, which like radio waves we cannot see with our naked eyes, but they exist. A torus is the electromagnetic field around all things; plants, people, planets, and even galaxies emit them. A torus has a midline or pole with positive and negative forces in combination with outward and inward energy flows. The flows result in a subtle force and pulse, all around everything.

The flow rates likely vary widely across the universe, but here on Earth everything is set at the same basic flow or pulse. There are natural fluctuations of course and entirely unnatural exceptions in the case of many modern inventions, but everything on Earth vibrates at more or less the same rate. People are dependent on the pulse of the planet Earth for our health and wellbeing. We are part of and dependent on the environment, not separate from it. As living beings we are grounded to the negatively charged

Mother Earth and under the positively charged ionosphere, Father Sky. We are integrated with the energy flow of heaven and earth. This is no new age jargon or Taoist energetic rhetoric, but science that has been used and illustrated in meditations for millennia.

All life on Earth resonates at the same frequency as Earth's torus. The Earth's pulse or heartbeat is measurable as the Schumann Resonance. It is an extremely low frequency electromagnetic pulse that goes through the Earth and interacts with the ionosphere. The Schumann Resonance fluctuates, but was found to normally be 7.83 hertz. When we are immersed in an environment out of tune with our set frequency, the Schumann Resonance, we become out of balance and weakened, our Merkaba, torus, or electromagnetic field is thrown off beat and we operate out of tune and become ill. In order to be in The Zone we have to flow with the flow of our environment in every way, even ways we cannot see or sense immediately like being in tune with the extremely low frequency Schumann Resonance. Meditative movement tunes us in to our environment, often in subtle and unrecognizable ways.

People operate on subtly different vibrational levels as if the opposing fields of their Merkaba were spinning at different rates. We shift in and out of these states depending on the environment we are immersed in and our overall condition and perception. Such states are measureable through the electrochemical reactions in the brain. The basic state is beta. Beta state vibrates at 14-40 hertz. Alpha state is slower and smoother vibrating at 7.5-14 hertz. Theta is the more deeply meditative state vibrating at 4-7.5 hertz. Delta state vibrates at 0.5-4 hertz and is akin to deep sleep. And there is a hypothesized fifth state of which little is known called the gamma state vibrating at 40-100 hertz. Each state is necessary and each is state can be beneficial in one way or another. But the transitional zone between 7 and 8 hertz, around the Schumann Resonance, between Alpha and Theta states, is considered to be the most conducive to overall balance, creativity and awareness of self and surroundings.

When we are in tune and in balance the fire grows and the energy flows. Ignition occurs within and we become empowered with energy like fire. When we are happy, healthy, steady and strong our electromagnetic field expands as does our ability to give and receive energy as symbolized by the Merkaba, related in the torus and the depicted in the Schumann Resonance. The more in tune we are, the more balanced we are, the more balanced we become, the more we're in The Zone.

The Zone is where all artists and all athletes go to be creative and push the limits. The Zone is the meditative mind state of balanced harmony resulting in relaxed capability. Being in The Zone feels like you are equally rooted and yet connected to the light at the same time. Being in the Zone begins with being balanced and results in being empowered.

If the Merkaba were slightly imbalanced it would fall apart. The same goes for any microcosmic and macrocosmic formation, the same goes for all living beings intertwined with Mother Earth. When we are imbalanced we operate in discordance and we start to fall apart. When we are balanced and flowing with the flow our wellbeing is enhanced, we're in The Zone and we can better perform and even uplift and improve ourselves and surroundings.

Being in The Zone begins by being symmetrically balanced like the Merkaba and its harmonious counter rotational opposition. The Zone is the midpoint of balance, like the point where two lines intersect. And like chi and prana are the same energy, being in The Zone, being at the balanced point, leads to access of the same energy no matter if you're being artistic, or athletic, or healing, or in a meditative state for any another matter. Aligning positive and negative electromagnetic current leads to charge, balance leads to fiery energy in machines and beings. And as depicted in the image of the Merkaba, the physical and metaphysical midpoint of humanity is in our heart. Being in The Zone is being in touch with our hearts, where the fire within resides.

I have always pursued my interests in athleticism and artistry, seeking to be balanced in The Zone to enhance my creativity. I have always fought and scraped to better my physical capabilities, to stabilize my emotional and intellectual state in a distracting and polluted world which can upset steadiness and balance. I found the most powerful practices toward self-development not only correlate in form and function, but also enhance each other in multiple ways. The most valuable systems build and better the connection of mind, body and spirit with natural surroundings no matter the initial focus.

The 108 Steps to Be in The Zone is a compilation of information on rejuvenation and individuation to develop yourself and your surroundings through the metaphysical number 108. 108 is the metaphysical number of oneness, nothingness and infinity. 108 is the pinnacle of metaphysical numbers, and has been sacred in the East for thousands of years. 108 is reflective of our microcosmic connection to the macrocosm.

We live in an increasingly toxic environment, so much so that it impedes our individual health and development of our full potential, sometimes in ways that can be mitigated, mostly in ways that must be ceased. My definition of strength and how to apply it has changed and expanded over the years, but my mindset is the same; build and maintain strength, create rather than destroy, be mindful of the environment. There is no way to be in The Zone without consideration of the environment. As soon as you become strong your ideas concerning strength expand, just like graduating is not enough, just like passion develops into compassion.

I used to seek ways to rejuvenate, strengthen and meditate to develop myself, to reach The Zone, myself. But eventually I realized there is no getting there by myself, in the same way you can't be rich by yourself. Prosperity has to reach everybody. No matter how I uplifted myself, there is only so far I could go in a degraded environment. Ultimately we have to help others in order to help ourselves. Today uplifting and inspiring them to take care of themselves and their surroundings is an important matter of survival.

Everyone is different and so for everyone there is a different path to their own Zone. And yet at the same time we are all dependent on the same elements and we're all the same biological design. And because of postmodern decay we all must learn to flow with the flow and to dodge toxicity in the same way. The 108 Steps contains information on ancient techniques and new understandings to create steps to begin your climb to your Zone. And yet this information may not be all you require. You might need more information, everyone has their own path and I can only help with what I know. The Zone is the same everywhere, our outlets are all different. There are many paths to ascension. There are many doors to the house atop the mountain, but inside is the same energy. You have to find your own way on your own path to your own Zone and you have your own key to a door, but 108 Steps is a quality map of the mountain and of paths cleared prior.

The story of the Japanese samurai Musashi relates the idea that one should immerse oneself in studies as if in a womb and alternatively embark to challenge the world like a warrior in order to develop oneself. The samurai warrior philosophy of bushido points to the importance of humble devotion to training and honor in living, being in The Zone. Humble devotion is one of the most important aspects to self-development, in fact devotion to practice is often more important than the practice itself. The 108 Steps to

Be in The Zone is in the spirit of art and athleticism, in the spirit of Musashi, no matter what one's specific pursuits are.

My interest in literary art combined with a near obsessive compulsive addiction to snowboarding inspired me to seek to better myself. Snowboarding and skiing, or snowsliding is a lifestyle. Not because it's culturally significant in and of itself, but because of a calendar year only a hundred days might be suitable to slide and only thirty days might be optimal, so one has to be prepared for the occasion where everything lines up. It's a lifestyle partly because it's difficult to compare it to much anything else where so many variables are involved and because there is practically no other activity like it, where you can speed downhill, fly off jumps and drop off cliffs.

Snowboarding is a perfect complimentary activity to tai chi, chi gung and some yoga - for me. For others there may be other complimentary activities, like biking or running or yoga. The combination of soft and hard, or passive and aggressive practices is the important mix. There are as many combinations as there are interests. For me it was variously tai chi/yoga combined with primarily snowboarding, for others it may be meditating combined with hiking or whatever. Practice exertion and relaxation leads to quality being.

Both tai chi and snowboarding develop your balance. The soft, slow meditative movements in tai chi compliment the high speed intense movements of snowboarding. Tai chi theory speaks about the negativity of being double weighted, having your weight set on two feet when performing movements, with some exceptions of course, in order to be grounded. And in snowboarding you have to position yourself in a similar manner, always pressing on your uphill edge and depending on the conditions and terrain pressing on your tail or tip. If your weight is not positioned correctly your balance suffers and you'll catch your edge and crash.

Philosophically speaking when people do not have grounded perception they become hypocritical, easily swayed off balance by the opinions of other. Such imbalanced perspective and all out hypocrisy was coined doublethink by George Orwell. Standing with your feet in a way you're your double weighted is indicative of physical imbalance and doublethink is indicative of mental imbalance. Always try to stand with your weight primarily on one foot and always try to be grounded in your thinking in order to be better connected and grounded.

There are any number of ways to stand, perhaps the best way to do so is to position one foot pointed straight directly under you with your weight on it and the other out at about shoulder width pointed about 45 degrees. The weighted foot has about 80% or more of the weight. Generally speaking you are standing correctly when imaginary lines extending out from the heels and toes can go by or brush by the other foot. If the lines cross you're off balance. Perhaps the worst way to stand is with both feet pointed out like a duck, with your weight placed equally on both.

Tai chi theory is concerned about the precision of toe and heel placement and movement, and in snowsliding such micro management of force is equally important. Tai chi develops one's spinning power through practicing subtle movements meant to build spiraling energy and in snowboarding one develops spinning power so as to spin through the air over jumps and obstacles among variables that demand equal subtle control despite the force involved. Tai chi hints at developing one's power in order to be light on your feet and yet rooted to the ground. When you launch off a jump you have to be light on your feet and you have to be rooted to land smooth. Tai chi is beneficial in multiple ways and tai chi theory is applicable in multiple ways as well, not just to snowboarding, but to all activity and philosophy. At first tai chi and such meditative movement is applicable to physical and mental balance, then connection with surroundings, intuition and things that are mostly unpredictable. Tai chi and meditative movement can be used for martial applications, balance for snowboarding or carrying groceries, and most important for healing as well as philosophical grounding and spiritual comprehension.

Both tai chi and snowboarding, or soft and hard practices, develop an understanding of the subtleties of balance, one in a very relaxed manner, the other actively. And both taught me about circumstances outside their immediate scope. At first the components I learned about tai chi and other meditative movements were simply to develop my physical balance then I realized they helped my overall determination and focus. Eventually I found that my actions to stay strong helped me rejuvenate when injured and further the practices led to an increased interest in spirituality.

The 108 Steps can help anyone find balance and heal themselves. Whether spinning off of cliffs and shaking off the tumbles of failed attempts or simply seeking empowered balance to deal with the life's other precipices the 108 Steps has something for you. I conceived the 108 Steps for the development of physical, mental and spiritual being and hope that like tai chi and yoga, the 108 Steps will offer many different lessons, just like learning to snowboard brings you to the top of the mountain and teaches inspiration.

Once you climb to the top of the mountain and know the view you can't forget it. You can't go back to how you were before. Once you've ascended to the top of the mountain and gained personal strength, you don't look at the world the same. Once you've tapped into the outlet, you're in. Let this be warning: you could change yourself. The reason for warning is not necessarily because dealing with your new thinking or ability is difficult, but because of how others might react to your newfound understanding.

To tap into chi, it's said that at first you have to imagine it, at first you have to conceptualize certain ideas to coincide with certain movements and breathing. And that once you have tapped in, in part using your imagination, the power of focused thinking, you're in. Initially imagination is one of the tools to help tap in and then it becomes impossible to imagine the connection away. This runs contrary to postmodern thinking, where all must be proven before belief. The power of imagination and its ability to instigate connection to chi and healing specifically is exemplified through the existence of placebos. Placebos exist as sugar pills in treatment experiments because the power of the mind or chi connection, however you want to word it, is so powerful as to be a curative itself requiring simple instigation of imagination. Placebos are instigation through sugar pill imagination. The problem for many is that they want to experience the chi first before they believe it, however just like popping the placebo pill, you have to believe first and then you experience the chi, the healing.

Each of the 108 steps is simple requiring simple approaches or changes. Simplicity is beautiful and strong. And frequently simplicity is indicative of power not any lack of it. Living simple is better for you and less devastating on our surrounding, but living simply today, in a complicated and polluted world, is not always a simple task. Being in The Zone is being in tune with oneself and one's surroundings. And today our surroundings, polluted from the complex ways we live require we lead a more simple future. Meditative movements assist in developing one's balance and energy and I believe meditative movements assist individuals in dealing with the increasing environmental toxins. Many breathing practices obviously physically assist clearing the lungs for instance. No matter how tainted our air, water and food become, spiritual energy, chi, is always pure and cleansing.

My interest in self-development, my concern for the environment and disdain for conventional chemical/mechanical operations of medicine and agriculture inspired me to write the 108 Steps. The 108 Steps describes metaphysical development in a toxic postmodern world, how you can better yourself, your thinking and being. There are more like 1080 steps and ideas within, some primarily physical and some primarily mental, but each is helpful.

Because of the misdirection of society, the radioactive particulate and petrolithic gasses polluting totality we're integrated in, because we are indoctrinated into adopting toxic practices, I wrote the following 108 Steps. If the world were less polluted and less corrupted I would have presented 108 different steps, or I would have just stuck with a more poetic exploration of 108. Because the world is a postmodern polluted mess devastated by industry operating in opposition to nature, because the world is filled with people concerned with completing bucket lists instead of concern for the present or future, because everywhere is hollow of individualism filled by institutionalization, I formulated these steps.

The 108 Steps to Be in The Zone can directly elevate mental, physical, spiritual and natural wellbeing with knowledge of 108 and taking on the practices described. The symbolism of 108 presents millennia old inspiration for individuation and, I hope, the 108 Steps I formulated inspire as well. The most powerful aspect of the steps is they assist you to assist yourself, but the catch is you have to make it happen for yourself. The understanding of 108 and the elaboration of 108 Steps are helpful and powerful, but you still have to go forward yourself.

I was pointed to the sharp significance of 108 by a teacher of sorts who noted my propensity for questioning and exploring numbers and numerology, specifically the number 4. After stunning me with the 4 main aspects of Om, the 4 sounds and the 4 states of consciousness it symbolizes, he said, "Four indeed is special and unique, but 108, there is a highly significant number."

Metaphysically speaking 108 represents the individual connection with universal energy beginning with the breath. He explained how japa mala beads (basically prayer necklaces representing individual and universal connection) have 108 beads on them and that Yoga breathing theory states that humans take 21,600 breaths every 24-hours, in 60 periods of 360 breaths meaning that every 12-hours yields 10,800 breaths, a cycle representing our own set of inner mala beads, 100 x 108. And later as I digested it all I learned that the yugas, one of the oldest and most extensive and intricate measurements of time divides the cycle of time into 4 ages is based on 108 as well. Each age is a measured in years being multiples of 108. For example the Kali yuga is said to consist of 432,000 years, 108,000 X 4. 108 links time with breath and universal energy -prana or chi- with the individual. 108 links the macrocosm with the microcosm. The totality of 108 is astounding. In Vedic philosophy number 9 represents wholeness. It's said our eyes and our physical senses can understand 3 dimensions. Multiply the powers of each dimension and you get 108. Power of 1= 1 (1×1), Power of 2= 4 (2×2), Power of 3= 27 (3x3x3), multiplying 1x4x27, we get 108. 108 is a lot to fathom.

Being in The Zone is being energized with prana and breath. It is balanced capability and integration with our surroundings. Increasingly the planet's ecosystem requires that we all become more balanced, that more of us are more in The Zone, acting in unison with each other and the environment instead of in spite of it and in spite of ourselves. We have to become more conscious.

Ancient meditations have cleared a path through the dense mountainous terrain of consciousness, but we must clear our own way through the new growth of different times and different minds. In the same way the 108 Steps can be of great assistance, but it is up to you to go forward to the top. You have to find your own footholds on your own path and proceed at your own pace to the mountaintop and most importantly you must take the initiative. The 108 Steps offers insight, inspiration and assistance, but you have to practice yourself and take your own path to individuation.

"Adapt what is useful, reject what is useless, and add what is specifically your own."
~Bruce Lee

Allopathic Institutions and I

Being in The Zone is immediately recognizable and yet frequently unquantifiable. Being in The Zone sometimes feels like you are closer to yourself than ever before and sometimes feels like you're watching yourself from a distance, as if in a movie playing in slow motion. Either sensation however results in an intense feeling of connection and oneness with self and surroundings, where everything insignificant disappears, where all superfluous tangents melt away and where everything relevant in the present is comprehended instantly and acted on with calm, controlled intensity.

Being in The Zone is relaxed mastery of an activity whether it is writing music like Wolfgang Mozart, playing basketball like Michael Jordan, inspiring the world like Gandhi or just being like Ramana Maharshi. Ramana lived simply on a mountain in India and managed to affect the world by committing to do so. Being in The Zone allows one to create in calm confidence whether the creation is artistic, athletic, altruistic or aesthetic. Being in The Zone allows one to perform at the acme of excellence with grace. The Zone is meditative mastery without unnecessary exertion.

The ability to be in The Zone however requires training and development, physical training sure, but more significantly mental training. Being in The Zone requires a journey and as with any journey it begins by taking the first step. Occasionally neophytes will experience what it's like to be in The Zone, yet mostly the beginner's visit is brief exemplified by accidental amazingness. Being in The Zone often manifests as beginner's luck, but to be in The Zone at will instead of at random requires mindful training to the point of proficiency and beyond.

Different training methods are required for different applications of being in The Zone. If one utilizes being in The Zone predominantly for artistic endeavors different regimens are needed compared to those who seek to The Zone for athletic pursuits. And yet there are some practices which can assist everyone no matter their interests.

The 108 Steps can be utilized for all pursuits, including artistic and athletic interests, as ways to attain physical, mental and spiritual wellbeing, to begin to be in tune with the natural environment and yourself. You will not suddenly be in your own Zone simply by reading this, but you may recognize the route more easily. Finding your own Zone is something you have to do yourself. The 108 Steps to Be in The Zone presents processes that can develop mind, body and spirit, benefitting your performance no matter the specifics, but you have to take initiative. No matter your interests and pursuits, no matter your uniqueness, the following can be utilized by anyone for developing individuation and potential. I have used these practices and found them to be healing, rejuvenating and strengthening in multiple ways. The steps can help you balance health and wellbeing and expand your positive influence.

Taking the steps toward being in The Zone is an expansive procedure and is all encompassing. In the same way that fresh, organic and nutritious food is good for the body and the mind and the environment and the farmers, the steps which bring us closer to The Zone, are beneficial individually and collectively.

Individuals and Earth vibrate the same. Individuals and the planet share the same ratio of water and ocean water has about the same amount salt as our blood. What is good for individual beings is also good for the Earth beginning simply with the shared interest in water quality and the same resulting degradation from taint. All life on the planet requires the same clean elements, frequently in similar ratios as the planet itself expresses. But today there is practically no water untainted and no oxygen unaffected and therefore no being similarly negatively affected. We all are born into a world that is essentially on fire and, even though we didn't start it, we have to do something about it, individually and collectively.

In the Celestine Prophecy, by James Redfield, parental influence is explored. It's noted we are the combination of our parents and we either adopt or reject our parents' behavioral attributes. My father is a farmer and my mother was a nurse. I am the result of the combination of a nurse and farmer who were rebellious hippies walking to their own beat. We all are a combination of our parents and more broadly a combination of our mutual past. I had a tumultuous, but by no means tortuous upbringing and ended up living with my aunt and uncle for a time too, they are artists. I am a combination of my farming and nursing parents and artists. I am a Celestine child and The 108 Steps is a combination of these influences.

I assembled The 108 Steps to Be in The Zone to assist others in achieving the mind/body connection, to build spirituality and to lessen the environmental burden we all are faced with, because I am a nurse's son, a farmer's boy, and the adopted son of artists. The world needs more art, more agriculture in cooperation with the environment and definitely more healing as opposed to creating conditions which require healing through war and pollution. The aftereffects of war and pollution are very much like the worst karmic demons imaginable; hindering future generations in horrible ways long after the confrontation is over. We are all a combination of our mutual past.

As the son of a nurse and farmer it is painfully obvious that conventional agricultural and medicinal institutions do not operate in cooperation with or overall benefit to people or life. Today even growing and healing are dirtied by corporatized mechanizations of prioritizing profit. Our food is less nutritious, less healthful and more dangerous -grown with toxic fertilizers, pesticides and genetically modified to withstand such poisonous conditions. At the same time the predominant socialized allopathic medicinal system increasingly utilizes toxic and poisonous methods of healing. The pharmacological concoctions used for everything from sleep disorders to 'unacceptable' behavior, the radiological cancer treatments and the entire cut and remove methodology of conventional modern medicine is as toxic and offensive as modern corporate agriculture.

Conventional agriculture has resulted in the promotion of near monoculture. There are fewer and fewer varieties of tomatoes, wheat and corn. The reason there are fewer crops to choose from in the stores and the reason conventional growers choose to grow one type of crop is because they found the crop with the most yield by weight. Even though the crop is less nutritious and even though we need an assortment of foods to be healthy, one crop is grown so as to better profit.

Conventional medicine operates in the same formation, primarily supportive of the institutions, not the individuals. Conventional medicine operates in the same one size fits all routine as conventional agriculture. For instance, the administration of pharmaceutical concoctions for a specific set of symptoms might only be determined by age, weight, sex, symptoms and past illnesses without thorough cause and effect investigation of the individual. The monoculture of modern agriculture and one size fits all approach to modern medicine benefits institutions not individuals. The corporate agriculture and corporate care both have some quality aspects, however profit has infiltrated and deformed aspects of sustenance and treatment.

Farming and healing both require one act intuitively to surmount obstacles that come together in a unique time and place. Both frequently require guesswork and specific exploration rather than operation on overall guidelines. There are indeed so many variables involved in the natural and biological world that there is no way to quantify everything involved in growing and healing besides using intuition. Doctors operate very much through educated guesswork. The conventional toxic growing and healing methods not only use poisons, but omit the value of intuition and alternative methods. The importance of intuition cannot be discounted or omitted, all farmers and healers have utilized it for millennia.

My parents, an RN and a farmer taught me about birth, life and death. I learned by eating animals I watched be born, that I fed and the vegetables I helped grow and harvest. And I learned in seeing my mother work in hospitals, hospices, clinics, emergency rooms and a medical insurance company. I learned about the power to grow and assist and about human frailty and mortality.

I learned a lot from my parents, directly and indirectly. My mother was a healer who wanted to at the very least alleviate the suffering she encountered. And now with hindsight I can say that the modern allopathic medicine institutions she gave her life to and entrusted with her life, failed her and actually caused her undue suffering.

Modern medicine failed my mother and enhanced her suffering. A misdiagnosis changed a minor injury to life changing paradigm. She was misdiagnosed, mistreated and then had to endure several surgeries to correct the malpractice, including insertion of a large prosthesis. The prosthesis was the end result of what should have been just a simple broken collarbone. The ordeal left her in constant agony and limited use of her arm. The pain led her to seek medication for pain and further medication for retreat from the resulting depression enduring such constant pain can cause. The idea of cut and remove, prescribe and numb, the very driving theory behind modern socialized allopathic treatment, does not sit well with me. The practice essentially cut and drugged my mom to the point where suicide became an option; and she took it. Modern medicine can be highly effective and can be a cruel failure compared to available less invasive options.

People in the medical field commit suicide at alarmingly high rates perhaps only comparable to and surpassed by suicide among combat veterans. Focused studies are elusive, but it's possible such institutions are painfully stressful and traumatic resulting in such decisions. It's also possible those in the medical field know exactly what kind of lousy road is ahead of them and opt out. I don't mean to exclude the personal and individual events which lead to suicide. I just want to focus on the big picture, for it's more telling. In fact being able to look at the big picture took a long time. The overall harmony disruption of modern medicine is comparable to combat.

The one size fits all allopathic cut and drug procedure removed a broken part of my mom and ultimately killed her or weighed her down so greatly that killing herself became an option, as it has so many. And for my mom who suffered malpractice as a Registered Nurse, who followed the most uncaring surgical instructions and took the most dangerous medications, the dark irony of the system failing her is stark. The allopathic medical system she devoted her life to, failed her. Allopathic treatment can be so destructive it burdens one with a lifetime of pain.

Allopathic mistreatment cost my mom her life just like allopathic philosophy killed homeopathic preventatives and curatives. All my mother ever wanted to do her whole adult life was heal and alleviate suffering and she was grinded down by the cutting and drugging of modern medicine to the point she could no longer be a healer. Modern medicine has its place, however it is not the only way or best way in all circumstances. Often allopathic procedures lead to prolonged suffering whereas homeopathic treatment and healing practices alternative to the American Medical Association model are noninvasive and often highly effective.

Homeopathy allows and promotes conditions in which the body can heal itself so as to prevent prolonged suffering. Allopathy cuts, removes and numbs. The discrediting and elimination of homeopathy and alternative healing was instituted not to enhance the livelihood and wellbeing of individuals through extensive surgery and prolonged prescription, but to line pockets. There is no money in homeopathy, there is no money in promoting herbal remedies for instance. There is no money in turmeric, but there is loot in radiation therapy. Allopathic treatment is where the real money is. There are many forms of cancer as well as many cures, but the money is in the oncological status quo, not in vitamin c and turmeric. There is no money in promoting healthful individuals through simple means. It's all about treatment and often treatment to death.

"To learn who rules over you, simply find out who you are not allowed to criticize."
~Voltaire

The idea of mandatory health insurance centralizing signing on to be insured to fall in line with allopathic practice and insurance philosophy instead of promoting realistic integrative healthcare is hard for me to accept. For one it's mandating allopathic treatment, not nutritional, preventative or homeopathic options of any sort. And two; insurance institutions are built up instead of individual compassionate care. It's as if adherents to allopathic philosophy left behind some of the most fundamental medicinal understandings in order to support oligarchical insurance mandates.

"Let your food be your medicine, and let your medicine be your food." ~Hippocrates

"Medicine should do no harm." ~Hippocrates

Because of the farming and nursing backdrop of my youth, combined with a tragic inconvenient insider understanding that medicine is often an uncaring business instead of a healing practice, I have always, whenever possible, sought natural remedies and natural strength builders in an increasingly industrialized and toxic world. Because of the innate indigo inside me I have a rebellious nature. Perhaps I was born that way, but perhaps the farm in Maine, the hood in Manhattan or the spirit of the Mendocino coast cemented my inclination to walk off the beaten path. Perhaps because the medical institutions my mother worked for her whole life and that she trusted with her life coldly failed her I walked away in my own way. Instead of insurance mandates, the 108 Steps contains individual empowerments.

The 108 Steps to be in The Zone will assist you to assist yourself. It is a combination of exercises and practices which can help you better yourself and your surroundings. Some would say that the following practices are a waste of time. These same people would rather spend their time watching television. I have compiled nutritional and healing processes that some would label alternative practices the success of which is entirely random. The same people would rather pop experimental pharmacological concoctions for healing with no better percentages on benefits than actual sugar pills and potential of tremendously damaging side effects.

I dropped out of high school. I went back and did just enough to graduate and received my diploma on time, for what it's been worth I'm not sure. Later, I dropped out of college. Soon enough I became what some might call a professional dropout or at least as professional as dropouts can be. I went outside the box as much as I could. I left the urban rat race, fled the suburban subdued society and moved to the mountains. I became addicted to snowboarding. Snowboarding and skiing or just snowsliding is one the most magical activities difficult to compare to much else. You can slide fast and fly through the air all while standing still on a board or boards, like a magic carpet. Snowsliding can be a Zen activity. Being Zen and being in The Zone are as similar places as they are sounding words.

Zen, originally a Buddhist sect, means absorption or meditative state. Snowsliding allows you to stand seemingly still and let gravity take you downhill at speeds routinely over 55 MPH. You can jump off cliffs of great height. You can perform acrobatic feats on all sorts of obstacles. You can soar and then land without shift or skip onto smooth transition. With snowsliding equipment, a snow blanketed mountain becomes a whole new stratum where one can be like a cheetah or a hawk absorbed in the meditative state.

There are a million variables in snowsliding, but when the conditions are right, when you are in sync with yourself and your equipment, when you are physically and mentally strong, when you are effectively in The Zone, you can fly. There is nothing like jumping off of a cliff or spinning and flipping off of a jump, setting your board down smoothly in what can be graceful that high speed can seem like slow-motion controlled micromanagement of movement. There are few sports or activities as intense as snowsliding. To grasp and master snowboarding or snowsliding you have to learn relaxed intensity so as to appear you are not doing anything as you fly down the hill or through the air.

Snowsliding is physically demanding, of course. But no matter how in shape you are, excelling at snowsliding requires developing one's mindset too. To master, let alone attempt, backflipping off a cat track or spinning 720 degrees requires abdominal strength and steadiness of one's legs and back, but more important is strength of resolve. More important is commitment, confidence and awareness of every micro-variable that matters. Snowsliding is an intense activity requiring serious strength and commitment of mind and body in mostly subtle ways resulting in a lot of power with minimal effort.

"Fall seven times, stand up eight." ~Japanese proverb

Snowsliding began for me as fun distraction from the loss of my mother. It transformed into an outlet for training my commitment. It required I be physically and mentally strong. Eventually I got hurt which led me to seek healing and rejuvenation and in turn I found an interest in spiritual development and intuition. What were initially ways for me to stay strong transformed into ways to rejuvenate and heal because sometimes snowsliding changes from a slow motion dreamscape into an edge catch and the realization you were going 55 when you start a haunting tumble as if catapulted out of a washing machine. And as the saying goes on the mountains, which is just as true there as it is anywhere, 'If you're not falling, then you're not trying hard enough.' Falling and failure is routine, in fact you have to learn how to fall before you learn how to fly, leading to occasional mastery. Over the years learning how to build mental and physical strength, I also learned how to better heal and rejuvenate and then found an increased interest in meditation and heightened spiritual connection with self and natural surroundings.

I have included information on tai chi, yoga and other meditative movements, some philosophical and esoteric ideas and meditations to form the 108 Steps. It is easy to combine the practices of and ideas in tai chi, chi gung and yoga for they are all are part of the same mechanism to develop and maintain the power of self, and connection with one's surroundings. These practices are the same element, like water. Kalaripayattu originating in India is one such martial, internal, strengthening and healing art. The kung fu of Shaolin was brought from India by Bodhidharma, it's all integrated or integrative. Water begins as water and ends as water, yet it is rain, then a stream, then this river and that river and then inside you and then the ocean and ice and snow, then steam and rain again. And water, like the life essence of chi and prana strengthens and maintains life in all its forms. Like water all of these practices originate from the same place, and all of them lead to the same place; The Zone. Whatever the different labels of practice, whatever the nuanced style, all tai chi, chi gung and yoga build energy. Call it chi or prana or universal love or consciousness. There is nothing wrong with practicing many styles to find your own style or to learn what works best for you. In adopting many different styles one simply builds the energy in many different ways. And one learns what is powerful and correlative as opposed to what is superfluous and exaggerative.

Tai chi, chi gung, and yoga can be practiced together. In fact, in another time, perhaps they were all part of the same practice anyway, the same flow and then became like dialects of the same language. As long as you have a positive and humble attitude when doing meditative practices, essentially asking to be part of the energy stream, as long as you seek to be more powerful so you can do more good and as long as you mindset is benevolent you will receive benevolent energy. Rains, rivers and oceans converge and can all be utilized by life, as can multiple practices, as long as the waters and intentions are unpolluted.

I experimented with different diets, exercises, rituals and even various confidence mantras. I have found a variety of concise ways to better self and have a more positive impact on my surroundings. The most powerful of which develop all aspects self, the mental, physical, spiritual and natural aspects. Tai chi, chi gung, yoga are all demonstrably empowering on each of these levels. Quality diet is the same in that it's good for the mind, body, spirit and natural surroundings. The most powerful theories and practices work on multiple layers like the best healing.

On the mountain there is another old saying, or as old as a saying as a young sport can have, 'Snowboarding saved my life.' In pursuing snowboarding I found innumerable other avenues for self-development. In pursuing a sport of dropouts, becoming for all extents and purposes a ski bum, I found reason for learning, reason for becoming and reason for pursuing spiritual connection with myself, others, and my surroundings. Everyone can change and ascend, no matter how much of a knuckle-dragger they are. And the path toward change is always different, but everyone requires a little push or instruction or instigation. The instigation can be as little as information and herein is information I hope will instigate your journey to find your own way to your own Zone.

"The softest things in the world overcome the hardest things in the world." ~ Lao-Tzu

I wrote the Matrix of Four, The Philosophy of the Duality of Polarity as a metaphysical approach to raising and understanding consciousness through exploring the number 4. Numbers provide hints of relationships between different cultures in comparative ideas and more than that, hints of relationships between different subjects or metaphysics. Through numbers we can gain comparative understanding of metaphysical ideas. Numbers and numerology provide keys to comparative understanding like the symbol of the Merkaba and the ideas behind it.

Through 4 one can explore human consciousness in a sensible model. Through 108 one can glimpse the connection of the universal macrocosm and our individual microcosm in a deep way and better understand intuition. The celestial divinity of 108 is in itself metaphysical, a combination of scientific and spiritual correlations, making the numerological reflections that precede the scientific validations too uncanny to be coincidental. 108 hints at the power of intuition and its significance was likely first glimpsed via intuition.

The Numerical Significance of 108

"The most incomprehensible thing about the universe is that it is comprehensible."
~Albert Einstein

The illustration above is the Sri Yantra. A yantra, meaning machine, is like a mantra, only instead of a vocalization it is an illustration. The Sri Yantra or Sri Chakra is one of the most complex and well-known yantras and is considered to be a visual holy instrument or holy wheel. It is said to have been conceived by a yogi intuitively and yet is geometrically perfect. The image is formed by 9 triangles, and therefore sometimes called the Nav Chakra for 9. The 9 triangles are set in a way to form 43 triangles and 54 points of intersection, that with a masculine and feminine side reflect to make 108 points. It is said to be the supreme symbol in the development of auspicious consciousness as is sometimes called the raja chakra, the king or supreme chakra.

Visual yantras, vocal mantras and the connected physical practices of asanas and mudras (various positioning of body and hands) contain metaphysical ideas understandable on multiple levels and multiple applications. Yoga itself means union or yoke suggesting joining spirit and matter, individual and universal, masculine and feminine. Chakras are energy points where such metaphysical union, tantra, begins.

Meditative movement positions our mind/body/spirit in ways to allow that connection to occur. The Sri Yantra is a more divinely complex depiction of the Merkaba which can be seen in its core and in multiples. In fact it metaphysically represents the human body and is said to contain 111 aspects.

108 is itself, on its own, a raja yantra. The celebration of 108 began in India among Hindus long before Buddhism. The celebration of 108 is centric in Buddhism but was infused into Buddhism from Hindu traditions. All major Hindu gods and goddesses have 108 names, some have 1008, (in Islam interestingly there are 99 names for Allah, 9 short of 108) Hindu and Buddhist prayer beads or japa mala have 108 points, as do the prayer strings of some Chinese Taoists (divided into parts of 36) and Sikh prayer strings of 108 knots. Perhaps more significantly and primal is the representation of 108 in Vedic astrology. It's possible that Vedic astrological systems first suggested the divine harmony of 108 and that the astrological system was based on astronomical observations concerning the number 108 and not simply intuitive recognition.

In Vedic astrology there are 12 solar and lunar constellations, each is divided into 9 houses for each planet. 9 x 12 results in 108. There are also lunar cycles of four sets of 27 days, equating to 108. Through the lunar and solar dynamics, the two sets of numbers, 9 and 12 for the solar aspect and 4 and 27 for the lunar, 108 was perhaps initially celebrated as well as each of these numbers by themselves. It's said that using astrology one's entire life can be mapped out. Many cultures utilize astrological concepts as a way to indicate one's character. Many cultures, especially in and around India also believe in reincarnation, the idea of which can be abstractly expressed in 108, when one dies one returns to nothingness and is eventually reborn into the infinite.

With origins difficult to calculate and trace, its significance was in all likelihood initially intuitively and astronomically recognized. It's clear the celebration of the number traveled with Hinduism, Vedic astrology and Buddhism and its original 108 canonical texts, but its exact origins are difficult to be sure. No matter the variation of the theological or philosophical constructs 108 was always regarded as the ultimate number of metaphysical divinity. Sanskrit is considered to be a universal and spiritual language, its sounds reflecting universalities and it contains 54 letters, each with a masculine and feminine variation, equating to 108.

The combination of 1, 0 and 8 represents the metaphysical connection of the macrocosm and the microcosm of god or universal energy with individual consciousness in the combination as oneness, nothingness and limitless, 1, 0, 8. And yet if this was the totality of it all 801, 081 or 180 could be equal alternatives. But 108 is the divine number. Partly because it is an ancient idea and partly because it corresponds with so many subjects, astrology, theology, philosophy, mathematics, astronomy and even physical practices its origins are difficult to trace.

The base ten numerical system used today originates in India as does the concept of zero. In numerology integers can be simplified by breaking them down and adding the individual parts. For example: $1 + 0 + 8 = 9$. 9 is said to be the number symbolic of the Earth goddess and humanity. Interestingly enough in 9 days there are 216 hours, which is 108 x 2 and breaks down to 9 too as $2 + 1 + 6$. One of the extreme initiations, tests of devoted meditation occurs on Mount Hiei in Japan where one the running monks as they are called run while fasting for 216 hours. 216 happens to equate to 6x6x6.

Mathematically speaking 108 is regarded as a harshad. Harshad is Sanskrit for an integer divisible by the sum of its digits, 108 equates to 9 for instance. Harshad also means great joy. 9 is unique in that 9 multiplied by any number can be broken down back to 9 in the traditional simplification of numerology. For instance: 9 x 12 = 108... 9 x 53 = 477...then $4 + 7 + 7 = 18$ and $1 + 8 = 9$.

This uniqueness of 9 is not 9 itself, but the fact that 9 is 1 less than 10 in the base 10 mathematical system. However, 9 does represent an unchanging unique formation physically, as well as numerically in the base ten system. In order to depict and cover all points of a space the most effective manner is to utilize 9 points. No matter the shape involved 9 points covers entirety and allows depiction and understanding of 3 dimensional objects. Imagine 1 point as the center and then a double cross intersecting at that point extending outward to 8 points, 4 corners above and 4 below. This idea can assist in understanding many ancient symbols, as all were two dimensional depictions on flat surfaces of 3 dimensional ideas. The depiction of the Vitruvian Man, the extra appendages along with the circle and square, are suggestive of this concept, as well as the squaring of the circle. Every flat depiction of meaningful symbols can be extrapolated into a 3 dimensional ideas using this concept.

Metaphysically speaking one can use the 9 points idea to meditatively hold, increase and shield your space by imagining building your positive energy to radiate around you from your heart, representing your center point, or just in front of you, extending out to cover 4 points above and 4 below. One can imagine the points as roses or lotuses or chakras or just points of light energy.

The following series of mathematical operations makes 108 what is termed a hyperfactorial. 1 to the first power = 1. 1 x 2 to the second power = 4. 4 x 3 to the third power = 108. This is a numerological abstract and yet it is the result of a somewhat beautiful series of operations.

Aside from the above equation some of other mathematical equations of 108 are: 2 x 54 = 108, 3 x 36 = 108, 4 x 27 = 108, 6 x 18 = 108, 9 x 12 = 108. 72, 3/4th of 108, is said to be the number of JVWH, the four letter word for god, the tetragrammaton. Pentagrams coincidentally are formed with five corners, each at 108 degrees, 108 x 5 = 540, which is one and a half rotations, 360 and 180.

Wheel of Dharma

The Wheel of Dharma symbolizes Buddha's teaching continuing to spread widely and endlessly. The eight spokes of the wheel represent the Noble Eightfold Path of Buddhism; right view, right thought, right speech, right behavior, right livelihood, right effort, right mindfulness and right meditation. Each of the spokes is at 45 degrees and every multiple of 45 breaks down to and equates to 9 in a mathematically beautiful way, with the center as the ninth point, extending endlessly. Such crosses are common throughout the world often in representation of a calendar year. 108 is as mathematically beautiful as is 9 and simplifies down to 9.

108 is symbolic for cosmic connection and represents integrating processed to reach the connection. It represents the union of the Earth mother, the sun, the moon and ourselves. 108 is symbolic for the number of steps required to complete a process of

self-development and refinement in a metaphysical communion of the individual and the universal. Many Buddhist temples have 108 steps leading up to them, in a single flight or 2 flights of 54, or 3 of 36. 108 represents the number of steps to be in The Zone, to be in tune with our inner and outer worlds, to bring balance to the microcosmic system with the macrocosmic.

Each digit in it is significant on its own and in combination they are more so. It is composed of 1, symbolic for the oneness and singularity of self and further for god and truth. 0 symbolizes emptiness, nothingness and further nonattachment through completion of practice. And 8 symbolizes infinity and the eternal connection of all things. In a not so abstract 108 presents the idea of everything in unity, oneness, nothingness and limitlessness, one right next to the other. It further represents the trinity of time; one present, zero past and infinite future. 108 is metaphysically beautiful.

When the Buddha was born 108 Brahmans or priests were invited to his naming ceremony. And the Buddha is said to have left behind 108 auspicious footprints or steps. Buddhist, Hindu and Taoist prayer necklaces have 108 beads or divisors of 108; 16, 27, 36, 54. Some believe there are 108 paths to god and in contrast 108 human delusions or defilements and 108 types of lies, sin and desire. In Hinduism Lord Shankar describes 108 forms of meditation to Mava Pavarti. Kali is depicted as being encircled by 54 points of fire. There are theorized to be 108 feelings, 36 of the past, 36 of the present and 36 of the future. In Jainism, there are 108 virtues of five categories of holy ones; 12, 8, 36, 25, and 27 virtues.

There are said to be 108 Hindu holy sites in India. One of the Hindu Upanishads (holy texts) states there are 4 sections of 108 Upanishads, though there are over 200 accepted books of holy text now. In the 3,000 year old Indian epic Ramayana there are 108 offerings Ram was supposed to make. And Krishna is said to have danced with 108 maidens. Taoists relate the story of the 108 Stars of Destiny. The stars represent 108 demons which were banished and then ultimately came back as the very opposite, 108 heroes for justice.

Hindus, Jainists, Taoists and Buddhists celebrate 108 for numerous reasons and some, at least in part, because of the many mathematical constructs that equate to 108. 108 absorbs both odd and even numbers and is divisible by 2 or 3. The number three is considered to be the primal sum of the primal odd and primal even, 1 and 2. And in that way 3 represents the idea of flow and flowing movement.

We are part of the Earth and its relationship with the Sun and Moon. We are flowing in an ecosystem, flowing in the solar system, flowing in the universal system. Individual life on Earth and the Mother Earth as a collective Gaia exists thanks to a unique relationship between our Earth, the Sun and the Moon. We are the perfect distance from the Sun to provide balanced seasons, with the moon just close enough to deflect asteroids and gently sway tides. And both line up near perfectly for lunar and solar eclipses. This cosmic spherical balance is formed through a relationship based on proportions of the divine number 108.

The diameter of the Earth at the equator is 7926 miles. The diameter of the Sun is about 108 times that: about 865,000. The average distance between the Earth and the Sun is 108 times the sun's diameter: 93,020,000 miles. The average distance from the Earth to the Moon is 238,800 miles, about 108 times the moons diameter: 2180. The relationship of the Sun, Earth and Moon provide for all life and moreover all consciousness on Earth. And the size and distance between the familiar celestial objects are all in the divine proportion of about 108. Through this astronomical, divine and miraculous positioning, 108 is symbolic for celestial order and perfection, and our microcosmic position in the macrocosm.

The celestial relationship between the Sun, Moon and Earth is balanced in a ratio of around 108, the exact distances fluctuate during spherical revolution of course. So even though the Sun is bigger and farther away than the Moon they appear the same size from Earth because of size and distance in proportions of 108. This knowledge was only specifically and scientifically understood in totality recently, during the 20th century. But 108 was a celebrated number long before specific scientific knowledge of its cosmic relationship was established beyond intuitive recognition.

The fact that our astronomical position relative to the Sun and Moon is proportionally based on 108 and the fact that Hindu astrological systems and metaphysical understandings demonstrate the number is highly intriguing. The metaphysical union of both astronomical and astrological significance indicates the possibility the why it was so revered. Though it doesn't indicate exactly how 108 was originally understood. It's possible its divination was conceived at least partially through intuition.

There are 108 main acupressure or meridian points in Chinese medicine. As well there are 108 pressure points in numerous martial arts applications. These meridian points are related to the Indian idea of varman points totaling 108 as well and the likely source for further understanding of these metaphysical energy points. Some differing practices across time and place note slightly varying 108 points and some have differing presentations of the total number of points, as one might expect from say neighboring dialects, infused with ideas of other peoples or isolated from the ideas other peoples.

In the martial art form from India called kalaripayit, there are 108 strikes. And in the ancient Indian dance called bharat natyam there are 108 fundamental steps, each with a different hand mudra or position. The martial arts of India are considered to be the original movements which spawned the many forms of martial arts all over Asia. The knowledge of martial and meditative arts migrated from India along with the auspiciousness of 108. Many Egyptian hieroglyphics depict meditative movements suggesting the origins of martial and internal arts can be traced back to ancient Egypt the land of khemet, where the word alchemy is derived from and where so many other concepts and creations originate.

In the Goju-ryu discipline of Karate the ultimate kata, or form, called Suparinpei, literally means 108 hands in Chinese. Other katas are named after other factors of 108. Yip Man, Bruce Lee's teacher, at one point developed a system of 108 strikes utilizing a wooden dummy.

The martial art of Muay Thai from Thailand is said to have originally had 108 moves before the influence and changes of Westernized boxing techniques. In yantra yoga, an ancient Tibetan form of yoga, there are 108 meditative and breath coordinated movements in all. There are 108 movements in Wu, Chen, Chu, Yang and Taoist styles of the tai chi long form. Many simplified forms contain just 8 elemental movements. Tai chi is often called the dance of death and all styles can be traced to the same source

More than likely it all begins with th 108 karanas in Shiva Purana's Tandava or cosmic dance. Each movement can be employed in exercise, combat and meditation. Many of Shiva's cosmic dance poses are used in Yoga, Kalaripayattu (possibly world's oldest martial art) and kung fu.

Most martial arts and internal arts are made up of both confrontation applications as well as meditational applications. Tai chi is the perfect example of this dualistic combination. For no matter how many fights one finds oneself in the greatest confrontation is an internal battle to develop and control the self and be meditative. The 7th form taught in Kuk Sool Won translates to the '108 technique' or 'Eliminate 108 Torments' form corresponding with the overcoming of the 108 Buddhist torments or defilements.

Many yoga practitioners celebrate performing 108 sun salutations on the solstices. There are said to be 7 main chakras and many other chakras. Chakras are simply energy points where many meridians, nadis or energy lines intersect. The heart chakra is considered the fourth chakra, the center and potentially the most powerful chakra. There are said to be 108 main energy lines which connect at or rather emanate from rather the heart chakra. Through the number 108 connections between many distinct energy practices are revealed as dialects of the same universal language from tai chi to yoga, Buddhism to various Hinduism, to Vedic astrology. Some Hindu beliefs speak of 72,000 nadis, whereas other yogis and Tibetan Buddhists point out 84,000 nadis in our bodies and correlating 84,000 yoga asanas or positions. Tibetan Buddhist physicians further note that we can become sick in 84,000 ways.

Our celestial position in the solar system is linked through a dynamic of 108. And some of the most ancient celebrations contain an intrinsically understood mention of the metaphysical importance of 108. It is a celestially divine, traditionally celebrated, theologically revered and mathematically poignant number.

108 represents the perfection of the size of, and the positioning of Earth in relationship to the sun and moon. This near exact dynamic of 108 results in the extraordinary solar and lunar eclipses where the sun and mon appear nearly the same size.

Through meditation and prayer, such as reciting mantras 108 using Mara beads or ringing a bell 108 times to mark a celebration as done by some Buddhists variously, 108 is representative of processes to reach refinement, for individuation in connection with universal systems. In contrast there are 108 processes of deterioration as suggested in the number of defilements in Buddhism. The microcosm reflects the macrocosm, and vice versa.

Yoga and tai chi arguably resulted from the same transference of knowledge that resulted in slightly different dialectical understanding of meridian points and different ways to energize them. Yoga, tai chi, chi gung and similar martial and internal applications are just different dialects of doing the same thing and all arguably resulted from the same transference of knowledge on the development of self. The potential proof of which is not only revealed in similar movements and breath work, but in similar reverence and reference of 108. In the same way that snowboarding led me to an interest in meditation and metaphysics through tai chi and yoga such practices may be focused on one element of building strength or spirituality or healing or self-defense, but lead to understanding and capability outside the original focus.

Information is knowledge, understanding the significance of knowledge creates power. The best information builds in multiple formats and the most valuable information correlates in multiplicity. The pinnacle systems of physical development for instance lead to increased development of and connection with the mental and spiritual aspects of self and ultimately being in tune with one's surroundings or being in The Zone. The 108 Steps represent a combination and a culmination of correlative knowledge which will develop all aspects of self. The 108 Steps will assist you in the development of wellbeing and potentially heighten your perceptive ability.

Humanity is malleable. We can develop or be developed. We train or are trained. Be sure one or the other process is taking place. When we are not training, you think you are steady at best or stagnant, but when you're not training, you're being trained. Society and the status quo will train you if you don't train yourself. And society needs change, not more people trained by society. When you're not training, you're being trained.

Rarely does society inspire compassion for instance, self-development including meditation does however. Meditation has immediate beneficial results. At first meditation and meditative movement can be felt physically, as if our load is lightened and our burden lessened. And eventually it is as though meditation can remove all our baggage and lighten our whole being so we are more capable to the point we are able to assist with load of others now and again.

Seeking to be a strong snowboarder led me to seek spiritual ascension of my own mountain which allowed me a better connection with myself, others and the natural world. I am not a master of tai chi, chi gung or any form of yoga. I rarely was the best snowboarder on the mountain or basketball player on the court. I hardly ever was the fastest and I practically never was the strongest or most limber. And I certainly need to meditate more often than I do. Further if I'm intelligent at all it is for realizing my ignorance. Yet I find I am observant and absorbent and can explain the subtleties I sense decently enough. I also have a decent memory and the ability to compare and correlate what I've learned enabling me to filter through chatter in order to find shared essences. I have learned a few things many people do not know, some of which have been kept secret or ignored, and I enjoy sharing. These following practices allowed me to better understand the essence of 108 and helped me to gain and occasionally maintain balance, and being in The Zone. For me the search for balance began physically in the development of my snowboarding skills. It expanded into mental development in order to focus and hone the mind body connection so as to commit my skills. This provided the impetus for spiritual development, which increased my concern for the environment I am in and am a part of. Life is self-development. The best things in life lead to development of all aspects not just the focus. For me pursuit of the dropout sport of the highest order led me to ideas completely unrelated to snowboarding, but relevant to climbing the mountain of self-development. Snowboarding saved my life and I want to share what I learned climbing the mountain, though we all go our own way.

I don't do every one of the 108 steps every day, but I do all of these things often. Each has helped me harness and maintain my physical, mental and spiritual balance, my resolve in a world negatively impacted by the toxic runoff of the pursuits of the status quo. All we can do is be aware and attempt to develop ourselves and better our surroundings.

Healthy surroundings results in healthy beings. There used to be only so many sicknesses and diseases that ruined mortal man. For every set of symptoms there was a particular problem which resulted in the dis-ease. Because of new factors there are now new diseases. The world has been changed. The beginning of the nuclear era of detonations and meltdowns coincided with the beginning of the cancer era. Combined with global burning of oil and coal, introduction of petroleum sourced plastics, heavy electromagnetic pollution and genetically modified organisms as crops and "conventional" agriculture as a whole and you have an altered and degraded environment. Now practically all waters are polluted with metals, pharmaceuticals and industrial particulate of every imaginable sort. All these new environmental factors result in new diseases and increased frequencies of diseases.

Studies found that the introduction of lead into gasoline and paint resulted in wide spread behavioral changes noted by an increase in violent crime in the countries where lead was introduced and a decrease corresponding with its elimination. There is acute lead poisoning and other acute killers brought on by our toxic ways, but there is also more subtle poisoning, like lead induced violence. The polluting factors are that intricate. We are permeable to influences that are detectable and untraceable.

All consideration of nutrition and health are behind the times if they are simply speaking of carbohydrates and fats. If they are not mentioning the toxicity of our environment and the lack of quality food and clean water available, the results of the global burning of petrolithic and nuclear fuels, they are not considering the present. The environmental degradation concerns us all now as well as the future of our offspring. So instead of bucket lists, wake up. The toxic runoff is confronting, affronting and devastating to you and the unborn of the unborn. There is no way to be in The Zone without consideration of the natural environment that is our home. You can't just go with the flow, one must flow with the flow.

I hope The 108 Steps to Be in The Zone helps you develop your mind, body and spirit and inspires you to redevelop your surroundings. And I hope these life lessons are as valuable for you as they have been for me in my pursuits to live well and expand wellbeing. Peace.

08 Steps

1. Sleep well, wakeup slowly and deliberately. Open your heart before your eyes. The heart is our midpoint where many believe there is microcosmic metaphysical fire, a spark of life within us. Be grateful and visualize positivity during the day's plan. Rise from sleeping without doing a tremendous sit up. Don't sleep more than seven hours unless you are hurt or sick, extraordinarily tired from exertion or are catching up on lacking sleep. Around six hours or less is all the sleep a balanced adult requires. Try to sleep on your side or on your back.

The expression 'sleep on it' suggests that one relax and let the solution to a problem come to you in your sleep. To enhance the potential that sleeping solves problems try practicing biphasic or polyphasic sleep. Biphasic sleep patterns (four hour sleep session and a lengthy nap) can ignite the same insights as polyphasic sleep patterns and is a lot less difficult to initiate compared to one long nap of an hour or two combined with a few short naps (approximately half hour long naps) throughout the day.

When one first enters the unconscious sleep cycle and experiences R.E.M. one's mind is open and easily focuses on whatever dilemmas one is facing in waking life. And in sleeping more often instead of longer the frequency of R.E.M. and lucid dreaming increases. Lucid dreaming is said to lead to elevated understanding and increased insights.

Biphasic and polyphasic sleeping patterns makes life more dreamlike and dreams more lifelike. Some of the most quality thinkers in history practiced taking several naps throughout the day instead of the customary lengthy session of sleeping during the night. Thomas Edison was one of many famous thinkers who practices changing their sleep patterns so as to be able to induce this transitional state between waking and sleeping more often.

When one first falls asleep one enters the dream state indicated by R.E.M., rapid eye movement. During this heightened mind state great understanding is possible and 'Eureka!' moments are frequent. Thomas Edison would work endlessly at his desk with a handful of ball bearings. When he finally fell asleep the ball bearings would drop to the floor and wake him up right when he entered the dream state. He did so because he found his mind was most activated at this time. This is where the principle and expression of 'sleep on it' comes from. You can find solutions in your sleep.

Changing sleep patterns can lead to finding solutions and heightened awareness. Learn lucid dreaming. Wake up after a few hours of sleeping and read or meditate for ten or twenty minute. Go back to sleep and focus on the lucid control of the dream state. Remember that it is only a slight change of consciousness between lucid dreaming and lucid waking. Awareness of your dreams is possible and can lead to possible betterment of your waking life.

Look at the palm of your hand during the day and before you go to sleep as you do so think about what you want to dream about. Throughout your day look at your hands and ask yourself, 'Am I dreaming?' The habit will manifest itself in your dreams and you can then take control of the dream. Carry something odd in your pocket. If you ever think you are dreaming, check your pockets. This can instigate control. As we age, beginning when we are teenagers, it becomes more difficult to lucid dream. It also becomes more difficult to imagine and dream in our waking hours as we enter adulthood.

Dream and follow your dreams. Hone, refine, enhance, learn and do whatever it takes to follow your dreams. Never let anyone destroy, shift, alter or eliminate your dreams and at the same time allow your dreams to change and transform like your tastes in music or beverage.

Find your dream, make your dream. Don't follow the dreams of others. No matter if it is a societal instigation or a particular person enticing your imagination, do not follow the empty dreams of others. Do not let others destroy your dreams in this way. Plan, believe, visualize and enact your plan. Elaborate and construct your dream into a viable operation and make it happen. There is nothing to it, but to do it. Follow your dreams and learn how to implement them for your dreams are from the heart and following your heart is one of the most difficult and rewarding pursuits the fruits of which are immeasurable.

Tibetan yogis and other yoga practitioners practice the art of dream yoga, the original lucid dreaming. About one third of the average person's life is spent sleeping. And in this time the majority of us are stagnant while doing so, idle minds barely aware of ourselves let alone the fact we are sleeping or dreaming. Before you go to sleep think positively and compassionately. The first stage to dream yoga is recognition of dreaming. The next step is transforming the dream and the third is known as multiplying. The fourth practice is to unify the dream with the clear light. Recognition, transformation, multiplication and ultimately unification of the dream with the light of the true self are the four essential stages of dream yoga. If you ask a question, if you ponder a subject for a time and do so while awake and just before sleeping eventually the answer will come to you in your dreams.

If you are experiencing insomnia, then meditate. If you are consistently having trouble sleeping then exercise more during the day. Pushups, sit-ups, calf raises and wall squats are all quick and powerful exercises. Wall squats are done with your feet flat on the floor and your back on the wall. Your thighs should be about parallel with the ground, never less than parallel. And as with most any activity, according to tai chi principles, your knees should be vertically above your toes. Always avoid bending your knees past your toes. If these processes do not help, try smoking or eating a tiny amount of marijuana. If you need to wake up early, drink two glasses of water or more. Do not eat and go directly to sleep. If you have back problems, occasionally meditate when it is your bedtime on the floor on nothing but the carpet of similar layer lying flat on your back. Occasionally sleep this way for at least part of the night.

Yoga nidra is the practice of yogic sleep. The point of yoga nidra is to link and enhance the dreaming and waking. It is essentially like focused napping. One can simply bring your attention to self, starting from the crown of your head and flowing to the tips of your feet and then returning attention back to your third eye as you rest your body completely still lying flat on your back and flex your awareness as you go in and out of sleep.

2. Try to floss your teeth once a day and brush at least twice a day. Occasionally rinse mouth with oil for a considerable time, up to twenty minutes or more, the oil and saliva attract bacteria -spit it out. Scrape your tongue. Use toothpicks to stimulate gums. Use toothpaste without fluoride. Fluoride is a bioaccumulative toxin, too much of which results in fluorosis. Refuse fluoride rinse at the dentist and moreover try to stop drinking it as it is added to many municipal tap water systems. Refuse mercury amalgam fillings. Refuse root canals, opt for a bridge. Reduce your exposure to dental X-ray examinations.

To the ancients the mouth was a major opening where good energy and bad energy could come and go. Modern medicine has proven that the health of the mouth is revelatory of the health of the rest of the body and that infectious bacteria can enter the body through the mouth and clog up one's system to the point such plaque contributes to heart attacks.

Chi gung, tai chi, yoga and similar meditative movements are often compared to flossing one's teeth. Flossing one's teeth cleans your teeth, strengthens the soft tissue of your gums and removes the invasive plaque in one's system. Meditative movements act in the same way, strengthening your bones, your ligaments and soft tissues and removing plaque from your system. Both are good for you in the similarly and the same little voice within us tells us we don't need to do them and similar practices.

3. Be present and in the moment. 108 as a whole can represent the present. The past is fixed like a column or 1 and the future is infinite like 8 and the permanent present is represented by the 0 linking and transposing the fixed past and infinite future.

Think of the number 108. 108 on a deeper level esoterically symbolizes the trinity of time. It displays the singularity of the present, the nothingness of the past and the infinity of the future. Just being in the moment can be incredibly productive and comforting. The solidification of the present into the unchangeable past can be upsetting, especially when we were not in the moment. Don't forget about the past, learn from the past, but don't allow the past to hold you there. The past is not you.

The past should have 0 weight, 0 burden and 0 grip on you. Imagine you have no confrontations or preconceptions from yesterday and you will find yourself in the present easier. Normally it's past failures and losses that leave a part of us stuck in the past. But even if what you did in the past was great, here is the present, waiting for you. Don't dwell on past failures or accomplishments. In fact to remove any burdens of any history, personally or collectively, one must not forget, but face the past so one can move on. To be present think of the number 108 where you accept the present and integrate it. 1 symbolizes acceptance, 0 symbolizes integration and 8 symbolizes transmutation the often sought after series of steps to harmony and relief; acceptance, integration and transmutation, 1, 0, 8.

The past is unchangeable and has led us here to this moment; the gift of the present. And from here and now there are infinite possibilities. Don't underestimate the potential of the future, that's like underestimating yourself. Mortals are presented with a limited time here to do what we may to clear the way for the future, Hindu tradition supposes that we all can live 100 or 108 years to do what we can. There is a finite amount of time, but we hold infinite potential in that period.

Carpe diem/seize the day and think about being infinitely creative in your problem solving. 108 represents the trinity of time, the oneness of the present, the nothingness of past and the infinity of the future. Value time, but do not let control you.

The divine cosmic significance of 108 was initially noted by observant and intuitive people thousands of years ago. Whoever intuitively recognized 108 the cosmic significance of 108 were in The Zone. Such intuitively recognized concepts, including the measurement of the speed of light are nothing out of the ordinary for the ancients and ancient Hindus especially.

Sayana, a 14th Century Vedic philosopher is quoted as saying, "With deep respect, I bow to the sun, who travels 2,202 yojanas in half a nimesha." This figure, of course, equates to just under 186,000 miles per second. Sayana did not come up with the information himself, but gleamed it from much older intuitively derived work. 108 has equally intuitive roots which are even older and harder to trace than measuring the speed of light at 2,202 yojanas in half a nimesha.

108 numerically displays the trinity of time, 1 being the singularity of the present, 0 being the weight of the past and 8 representing the infinity of the future. And like the Om symbol itself and so many other concepts, Hindu and otherwise, where there is three there is most often a fourth, the unspoken, the silent inexplicable. With Om, there are the A U M sounds and the fourth unsaid, that of silence, the silent

inexplicable. In the case of the trinity of time displayed in 108, the fourth part following present, past and future, the silent inexplicable is timelessness. 108 and Aum are related in this way and in that they are perfectly in rhythm with all of space and time.

The fourth aspect of time or by definition related to time, as suggested through the intuitively grasped idea of 108, is timelessness. 108 points to timelessness and reveals the key to understanding it too. Timelessness is a combination of the trinity of time and independent of each part as well. Timelessness is where intuitive hints exist and from where such intuition is gained. Glimpsing intuition, tapping into the timelessness of the Akashic field can only be accomplished by being present on its shores if you will. 108 represents the trinity of time we are all immersed in; the present, past and future. And its intuitive derivation suggests the fourth silent inexplicable of timelessness, where intuitive ideas such as many within 108 itself originate. In order to access timelessness one must be present, without preconceptions or projections from past experiences and be open to infinite future possibilities. Being present without the weight of the past while being open to the future can put you in touch with your intuition. This layer of 108 represents oneness, nothingness, infinity and liberation.

A specific meditation with the purpose of being present is called Shamatha. A variation of an old joke meditators is that being present is just about the easiest and simplest thing to do and is in fact next to impossible. To truly be present one has to shed oneself of all concerns for the future and all notions of the past. Sit in a chair or cross legged in a quiet setting without music. You can keep your eyes open as this meditation is about being present. Focus on your breath. As you are breathing your mind will wonder and when it does note so and return to focusing on breath. Be calm and allow the random thoughts come and go. When finished take this calming meditation on being present into your everyday life and interactions.

Your physical body is always present in the here and now. Your physical body is subject to time and space and is always here and now, always present. Your mind and spirit are not limited by time and space can traverse the past and the future and the expanse of all creation simultaneously, in fact we often are not present and without realizing we are not present. Meditation on the physical breath and meditative movements like tai chi, chi gung and yoga bring our mind, body and spirit together, into the present.

4. Meditate. Meditation and a meditative mind state is the pinnacle purpose of all yoga, chi gung, tai chi and any like internal art. All such practices operate in a progression toward a meditative mind through movement and all practices end in meditation for meditation is the very point, each time you practice and of the practice in total. Movement results in balance, balance provides centering for meditation. Meditation is focused absorption in self, idea or energy.

Meditate on your breath. Meditate on your breath so much that you are able to meditate on nothing else and ultimately nothing at all. Meditate for five minutes or less, just meditate often. Meditate on being aware, relaxed, peaceful and positive. Meditate on being calm. Meditate on being well. Meditate on simply being and on being simple. Meditate on having no thought or meditate on a single thought.

Perhaps the easiest way to begin a meditation practice and achieve a meditative state for a moment is to meditate before you sleep or when you are extremely tired. Do so by lying down flat on your back with your hands cupped (right on top for men, left on top for women) resting on your lower belly. Bring your knees up so that your feet are resting flat on the surface you're lying on. The trick to meditation is to meditate, just as the trick to walking somewhere is to take the first step. Everyone has a trickster within that can convince us not to begin. All you have to do is start walking.

Sometimes after a rewarding and relaxing meditation session I will be so relaxed that the trickster-mind finds ways to be relevant by activating concerns or worry. The trickster or ego or what have you can be so disturbed by the meditative mind state that when I begin to settle back this part of me will literally press the old standby panic button and ask, "Wait, where are the keys? And what about your wallet? Aren't you late?" Do not let your ego eliminate the meditative mind state when you gain it. Take the ego and let it go. The worst mind trick is when we convince ourselves not to meditate you into not beginning meditation at all. Remember this to overcome the trickery: meditation does not take time, meditation makes time. Meditation leads to longer more healthful lives and being more capable while alive also enhances us so we require less sleep.

Meditation benefits circulation, is good for the heart, increases response time, enhances empathy and improves observational skills. Meditation has been proven to assist in breaking addiction, curing depression, alleviating stress, improve ability to maintain calmness in stressful environment, ease chronic pain, cure insomnia and even reduce the blood sugar of diabetics. Meditation can slow the aging process, though there are no definitive scientific studies proving this, just examples of those practitioners. When we are not addled by stress we can live easier.

Awareness of breath is possibly the most important aspect of meditation. There are many forms of meditation practice that coordinate different abdominal movements with different breathing techniques mindsets all like different keys to different doors to the same building. However all forms of meditation contain the following primordial elements. There are four parts of every breath; inhalation, pause full (~85% capacity), exhalation and pause empty. Take a second or two to be in the pauses. Being attentive of a breath cycles of about 8 seconds inhalation/exhalation and 2 seconds pause full/pause empty is a good way to be aware of and slow the breath. There are also four basic aspects of meditative breathing no matter the variation; breathing slowly, steadily, deeply and consciously. One trick to focus on the breath is to bring your attention to one point. In the beginning of practicing focus on the tip of your nose where the breath originates, as you meditate more or for longer focus your attention on your diaphragm. Try to imagine initiating the breath not from your lungs, but from below you belly button.

There are four basic forms of body positioning for meditation; sitting, standing, lying down or walking. There are also four forms of mental positioning for meditation; focusing within with clear mind, focusing outside oneself with a concept in mind, focusing within with a concept in mind, focusing outside of oneself with a clear mind. The more one can clear one's thoughts/feelings the better one can clear tension and unease. The more one can focus on a thought/thing the better one can solve problems and unease. Initially focus within with a clear mind. Then try to focus outside of oneself with a concept in mind, a search for the solution to a problem for instance.

Meditation should be done in a comfortable position, but not too comfortable. One should be relaxed, but not so relaxed that you fall asleep. Of course if you fall asleep it's alright. Meditate sitting cross legged, meditate in a chair or meditate in the corpse position, lying flat on your back. Place your tongue on the roof of your mouth, do not clench your mouth shut, but you may place your teeth together or near. Breathe through your nose. Try to stretch or do tai chi, chi gung or yoga before meditation, but you can meditate anytime.

People spent lifetimes researching meditation thousands of years ago. There is an endless stream of information on different meditation practices. The correlations of the many meditation practices are vast. Some of the most powerful correlations as basic as it may sound is to imagine your core rooted the fiery core of the earth. And to next imagine being attached to universal light energy through you're the crown of your head. Then imagine gentle circular intermingling of earth and universal energy.

Meditation rids one of tension however it is sometimes important to actively bring about a relaxed state as one meditates. One must actively quiet and relax the mind, body and breath. The shoulders are stressed the most among men and the hips for women, both hold tension in the chin and shins. Think about relaxing the tension you are aware of and think about relaxing the tension you are accustomed to and do not notice as much because of the long term presence. Think about ridding yourself of thoughts which can contribute to or be outright causational of tension. Such thoughts might be immediately recognizable as such and others might have accompanied you for so long they might be harder to find.

One of the easiest ways to begin to meditate is to think of 108. The magnificence of 108 is incomparable to any number in the meditation equation it represents alone. Begin to meditate thinking on 108, not the entire complexity of it, but just the meditation equation of it. 108 is the formula for beginning meditation and understanding it, a short numerical guide.

Meditation begins by focusing on 1 point in the environment or one thing, most frequently your breath cycle. Focusing on 1 thing enables us to eventually focus on nothingness or 0 things. Focusing on 0 things, the ability to be clear results in parallel increases in energy and relaxation and enables people to focus on the infinity, symbolized in 8. 108 is the number on how to meditate. Practicing the meditative process of 1, 0, 8 can lead to powerful meditations on its own. Try meditating on 1 thing many times, it can be a different thing, though breath is the simplest and perhaps best 1 thing to focus on. After practicing meditating on one thing, then try thinking of nothing. After meditating on these two parts practice including the third step, focusing on the infinite. Of course masters and gurus, people who practice meditation often go practically straight to the infinite.

108 is the meditative process simplified, 108 is the common denominator of meditation. Most people spend most of their lives not focusing on one thing, but rather

chatterboxing about in distraction mode, the mind unfocused on many things and nothing. The ability to focus on 1 thing eventually enables us to focus on 0 things, each of these mind states are by themselves tremendously pleasing and empowering relative to being unfocused on many things. Ultimately the ability to focus on 1 and then 0 or nothing allows us to focus on the infinite. Focus on the breath and then try to allow clear everything so that you have 0 fear, doubt or mediated distraction within, enabling one to peer into the infinite. When you are able to focus on 1 thing nothing can distract you, you can let everything go and then tune into the infinite.

5. Learn and practice the Five Tibetan Rites of Rejuvenation. Be sure to do each Rite the same number of times. Start at 9, 12 or less if you are injured or unaccustomed to yoga or physical activity. Each Rite should be performed the same number of times for balance. 21 repetitions is considered the optimal number or Rites. With intention one can easily do 21 or more repetitions of each of the Five Rites of Rejuvenation. Doing more repetitions might give you more of a physical workout, but 21 times moves the energy properly and maintains its balance.

In between each Rite, stand straight with your hands at your hips and your feet together, or slightly apart, like Superman and take two deep breaths. Inhale through your nose and exhale through your mouth with pursed lips, in the shape of an O. Breathe in until around 85% lung capacity and out completely so that every bit of air is exhaled. Imagine inhaling positive energy and exhaling stale air.

Follow up the Five Rites with meditation lying flat on your back, palms facing up. One trick in pursuing meditation is to focus on the breath. Breath through your nose and think of only the tip of your nose. Imagine relaxing so much your body settles into the floor, the only part of your body activated are the tips of your fingers so as to keep you palms flat and settled down too. The longer you meditate afterwards The Five Rites or any meditative movement the more you benefit. Perform the Rites, or any yoga, tai chi, chi gung at any time, but most preferably in the morning, when the world is quiet, on an empty stomach.

Begin each movement with inhalation through the nostrils and return on the exhalation. Movement and breath should be slow, steady and performed in unison. The easiest way to count the Rites is saying the number to yourself as you inhale and exhale.

Rite One: spin clockwise with your hands active, palms facing down. The slower you perform each Rite the better. One way to do the first Rite is to simply spin, the other is to spin in coordination with breath, inhaling on the first 180 degree rotation, exhaling on the second 180 degrees of the rotation. Another variation is to hold your forearms up at 90 degrees, palms facing inward and spin in coordination with the breath, sometimes while looking to the right hand, sometimes not.

Rite Two: think about keeping your tailbone on the ground. Try to lift and return your neck and legs to the ground at the same time. All these positions should be done with straightness in mind, however do not lock your joints –ever, during any movement. If you can lift your legs slightly past 90 degrees do so.

Tai chi and chi gung principles insist one not strain oneself during stretching and treat it as just being in a position. Yoga practices often seek to settle farther and deeper. The Rites can be a strain, but you should not endure pain. Do them as best you can, as many as you can. Treat the Rites or any such practice as a walk. One does not have to traverse the valley perfectly, without stepping in one puddle or stumbling on one rock and one can still arrive at your destination perfectly.

Rite Three: set your knees about four inches apart and settle on your knees and the tips of your toes. Keep your hands just under your buttocks with your thumbs slightly grasped on the sides of your legs. Use your hands to support your movement. Bend back gently never straining to pain. When you return to starting position on the exhale go far enough so that you back is straightened. Initially requiring you bend slightly forward past 90 degrees in order to straighten back in this position. Each Rite can be seen as opposing the other in an abdominal dynamic. The Second Rite prepares us for the opposing third and so on.

Rite Four: set your hands at the side or your hips your palms facing forward, keep your arms straight and your ankles about four inches apart. Keep your ankles and hands in place –unless you need to adjust. This is often the most difficult Rite to master. The main initial mistake is moving one's shoulders and arms. Keep them straight in alignment with your back and at your hips. Inhale from there to a table without moving.

Rite Five: set your hands and feet at the same width, a little wider than shoulder width, keep arms and legs straight and in place –unless you need to adjust. Remaining on your toes lift and push up into an upside down V. Remember that after the Fourth Rite your muscles are ready to fire off in the opposing direction of the Fifth.

Add the Sixth Rite only when and if you are able to do 21 repetitions of each of the five. Begin with just one of the Sixth Rite. The Sixth Rite should only be included after practicing the Five Rites and the doing the full 21 repetitions without strain. It is not necessary to do otherwise. The Sixth Tibetan raises sexual energy levels for transmutation into life energy and is only done optimally 3 times as opposed to the other Five Rites. 21 repetitions of the Five Rites, plus the Sixth Rite done 3 times equates to 108 breath coordinated movements. See Step 55 for further information on the Sixth Tibetan Rite and transforming or raising sexual energy.

Tibetan yoga is extremely secretive because of its isolation and the tradition that information must be passed on from a master to qualified students. The Five Tibetan Rites of Rejuvenation may well be the first series of movements adopted and then interpreted anew in the outside world from the region though the Five Rites may more likely be of Nepalese origin. Like yoga from India and other internal and martial arts from the rest of Asia the Rites were likely transformed and integrated anew with changing times and interactions. The exact origin of the Rites is mysterious, but its power is obvious, the Five Rites offer condensed benefit and develop a lot of inner heat.

The Chinese have taken over and integrated Tibet and in the process they have killed, dismantled and homogenized a rich and compassionate culture. This has led to a heightened interest to learn and impetus to share Tibetan yoga traditions. The six forms of Naropa yoga are Tibetan yogi training traditions. Literal methods of the allegorical mountain wise men. The first is the yoga of inner heat or tummo, followed by the yoga of the illusory body, yoga of the dream state, yoga of the clear light, yoga of bardo (bardo is the stage between death and new birth) and yoga of the transference of consciousness.

The specifics of these practices are indeed too complicated to impart in any other way, but directly from master to qualified students. The movements in preparation and the mindset for qualification are so complicated that direct exchange of information and direct instruction is normally the only way. I say normally because the power of the mind can supersede anything including lacking instruction. However even the power of the mind requires practice, dedication and refinement. Today isolation of the mind in the mountains is nearly impossible. And when the mind is weighed down by stressors, simple or complex, more practice is required simply to attain a meditative mind state required to begin to gain the meditative mind state.

The Tummo meditation creates inner heat without movement. The basics of the complex meditation include meditating on being totally hollow. Imagine there is a fire within the heart that fills one with heat and stirs the three vertical flowing channels of energy coursing along the spine to glow and emit heat as well. The Tummo practice empowers the individual to the point that outside influences, including extreme temperatures, do not alter the mind state of the individual. This practice is what enables Tibetan yogis to live in solitude high in the mountains in extreme cold, but is about more than staying warm. For more on Tummo and the Five Rites in combination with chi gung see the ebook Tibetan Fusion.

6. Learn and practice the bone tapping technique of rotating on one's axis or ringing the bell. This basic warm up builds energy through the gentle rotation of your spine. Stand mindful of having your weight on one foot or your feet touching. Imagine as if you were armless and the action was originating in your dantien, the space just below your belly button where according to understanding of chi, all movement originates. As you go, imagine the movement is originating in your grounded feet.

Rotate back and forth so that your arms sway and tap your back and sides, your kidneys, adrenals, abdomen and lower back. Stand with your weight on one leg and change how they are touching as you go along, they can be next to each other or one on top of the other. You can try standing with your feet apart too, in combination with shifting weight from foot to foot, but just try to root yourself, connect with the ground through the balls of your feet. Tap the lower back and the kidneys lightly with your arms as you rotate. Further imagine your chi is moving you.

There are basically four aspects to ringing the bell, the lower, middle, higher and martial bell ringing. The lower is the most important one. The middle one is done the same perhaps adding a little more coil and a little more spin power. Do the same movement, only allow your arms tap or pat your lungs, heart, liver and sides. The higher form is tapping above your shoulders, arms, back of your shoulders and ultimately your collarbone. Maintain the same principles of being rooted as you do the middle and higher. The more martial form, perhaps the least important one to do, especially initially is done with more force, low, mid and high. The forceful taps or hits moves chi and dampens tension, however the lower form of ringing the bell is the most important.

Ringing the bell is one of the original, most fundamental and most valuable warming and loosening movements there is. It is primal, as are many tai chi and chi gung movements and easily integrated into any practice. You will note many young children performing this and other similarly primal tai chi and chi gung movements as if instinctually building their chi.

Look at your palms before doing tai chi or chi gung, Tibetan Fusion or just the axis rotational bone tapping of ringing the bell. Then look at them after twenty minutes or more. Late look at them after doing other exercise to compare. Chi can be seen and eventually felt in the palms. One will see one's palms go from one uniform color to splotchy. The more intense the splotches, the more chi is moving. The splotches that develop on the palms are from blood flow and chi flow increase.

7. Perform tai chi joint rotations slowly and steadily. Begin with your ankles. Rotate your ankles in a relaxed and focused fashion both clockwise and counterclockwise six or nine times each. Rotate clockwise first and try to move equally slowly and steadily. Do

the same number of rotations with your knees touching, feet together and bending slightly forward, press your hands on your knees and do slow rotations, always clockwise first. Keep your knees on top of feet, never going past your toes. Then do the same movement with your feet about shoulder width apart, inward circles first, easy and slowly. (Imagine there is a line coming straight up from your big toe. If your knee bends past that adjust back so your knees are above your feet, not past your toes!)

With your feet together do the same with your hips, slowly and intentionally. You can and should always rotate your hips more. Do not rotate so you put stress on your sinews, but with your chi or energy. Do small circles both ways and then large circles both ways with your hips. Thirty times or more is fine, you can never do too many of these as long as you are not exerting pressure. Medical chi gung will have ill people simply do these rotations for a half hour or longer.

Next rotate your wrists in the circular pattern, clockwise then counterclockwise, the same way, six to nine times, inward circles first. Next are the shoulders. Keep them in line with the spine and rotate without force, extremely slowly. You can vary this by using the opposite hand to light press on your chest so the movement is in your shoulder, not your chest. You can also have your hands slightly holding your hips as go, again so as to focus the slow, steady movement of the shoulders. You can also lift your shoulders up with an inhalation and then release them down on exhalation a couple of times, these completely relaxing shrugs release stress. Imagine stress being let out of all the gently opened and loosened areas. Finally rotate the neck, in extraordinarily small, slow and relaxed circles, clockwise and counterclockwise. Always be extra careful and attentive doing circles with your neck.

8. Learn and practice what is known as a basic eight form of tai chi. There are many different tai chi short forms containing eight or more movements. Like most yoga, tai chi and chi gung, the short forms and the associated long form movements are seriously complicated in theory and practice. They are nearly impossible to learn from a book without some prior understanding or instruction. Some yoga, tai chi and chi gung can be communicated via image and description, but the tai chi long and short forms are too fluid to be taught in a book. You will have to seek instruction for this and it's advisable to seek instruction if at possible to at least gain elementary insight –concerning all

subject matter. Once one has a certain level of understanding learning on your own is tremendously powerful.

You can easily learn the Eight Brocades or standing Eight Pieces of Silk on your own, though it demands understanding of concepts which, which with personal guidance can more refine the movements. The more instruction one receives the more one gains from static pictures and descriptions later. The Eight Brocades have been adopted, transformed and utilized by practically all martial and internal arts, from postured yoga to kung fu. The Eight Brocades can be done extremely slowly and meditatively or they can be done slowly with tremendous exertion or a combination of forceful varying speed with varying relaxation and tension. There are innumerable variations of The Eight Brocades and you really cannot do them wrong, but can endlessly refine them. They are indeed so primal and so simple as to be beneficial no matter what form you use and no matter the stage of your practice. Like so many beneficial practices they are simple to learn and yet deeply complicated to master, with layer upon layer of refinement possible.

Some of the movements of the Eight Brocades and simpler movements in tai chi have been adopted, even universally accepted among so many practices that it is difficult to trace their exact origins, likely because they are recognized as being capable of spurring large amounts of energy in a simple manner. The easier one can learn a movement without having to concentrate on every minute detail, the quicker one can settle into a relaxed mind state, a quality parallel for movement and obtaining potential benefit.

The more complicated practices however, like the long form of tai chi, can be beneficial even when one is clumsily attempting mimicry for the first time. Complex movements can be beneficial even when you feel like a clod while doing them, however the point is to feel graceful and capable so as to control and not just experience energy. Learning meditative movements can result in feeling clumsy at first, but even still can be beneficial. Of course a relaxed mind performing simple movements is likely to experience more benefit than a moderately tense mind attempting any movements.

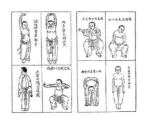

The above illustrations simply depict the Eight Brocades. The first four are in the left box beginning with the top right box with the overhead movement and proceeding downward and clockwise. The fifth movement begins in the right box and proceeds downward and clockwise the same. Repeat each the same number of times. Such movements, whether the Eight Brocades, the basic of eight form of tai chi or some other position or movement when practiced enough become yours and even though you can always improve your performance of them, they will always help you improve. And better still they become things you can always share and no one can take away. Many differing systems utilize the Eight Brocades differently. The following is just one of many variations.

The Eight Pieces of Brocade has been performed on its own and integrated endlessly. The form is utilized in chi gung and integrated into some Tibetan forms of yoga as well as Shaolin Kung Fu. The form is utilized as a standing practice and sitting. Like all tai chi and most chi gung the Eight Brocades can be done in a totally relaxed manner, slowly and meditatively slowly and intensely or rapidly or rapidly and forcefully. Either way the form is beneficial. Begin doing them in a totally relaxed manner. Repeat each one three, six, eight, nine, twelve, or twenty four times, only do each one an equal amount of times.

The Eight Brocades is a perfect example of a set of movements which has been endlessly integrated with other disciplines, is performed in innumerous variations in posture and even order, and yet is so simple and so effective that it practically cannot be done wrong and can be endlessly honed. Each is simple and effective and easily integrated, either directly or as familiar variations. One's mindset should be as a warrior in training. The warrior training you are undergoing is not a martial one, but an internal one. You should imagine, when the stance is obviously made for striking that you are striking and destroying bad ideas, the ego, stress and any negativity we all experience.

#1 Pressing Up to Heaven. Raise your hands above your head with your fingers interlaced on inhalation or the tips just touching. Including a bend from side to side in this position is an important variation. Bring your hands down to an unlaced cupped position at your dantien, fingertips touching or cupped, men with the right hand on top, women the left.

#2 Drawing The Bow and Letting The Arrow Fly. With your hands pointed with one or two fingers pretend to pull open a bow and release an arrow beginning with shooting to the left position then releasing and rotating to the left to pull the bow on the inhalation. You can imagine pulling a large bow of great force in slow motion then shooting an arrow into the infinite or at a target. On the exhalation release and bring your arms to a guard position, forearms next to each other . and rotating to pull again the other direction.

#3 Separating Heaven and Earth. This movement is similar to #1 only you lift one hand to the sky while press the other hand to the ground. Each wrist is active on reaching the top or bottom depending on the alternation each pointed inward.

#4 The Wise Owl Looks Backward. Stand with your feet shoulder width apart with your hands at your sides. While maintaining a straight back look to each side and up. With your right arm to to the left and reach up, alternate sides. Look to each side with your hands at your abdomen fingers touching. Then to each side with your hands interlaced behind your back.

#5 Big Bear Bends from Side to Side. With your hands on your needs rotate about 270 degrees, beginning in a clockwise direction as if a powerful bear. Alternate sides.

#6 Touching The Toes and Bending Backwards. With your arms lifted gently above your head reach up and back on the inhalation. On exhalation reach down to your feet and pull up you toes.

#7 Lifting The Pillar. With your feet together and arms at your side on an inhalation rise up onto the tips of your toes and bring your arms up, bending from the elbows so that your fists face each other at your belly, with your forearms parallel with the floor. Repeat

#8 Punching With an Angry Glare. Begin with your hands at your sides in horse stance with your palms facing up in fists. Punch forward on the exhalation with your left fist unraveling and rotating the fist so that it is upright just as you near the end of the blow. Alternate doing the same on the right side. Now punch to the left side using the same rotating unraveling peaking on the end of blow. Repeat on the right side. These four blows equal one set of #7. When you have finished however many sets you are doing raise you fists to the left, your palms facing you, with your right hand lower and behind your left. Breathe in this position for a bit imagining facing off whatever your foe may be, be it an inner demon or an actual tormentor in the form of a person or an adversarial affliction. Switch sides and face the right in the same manner with the same mindset. While punching think of expelling some of the energy you just summoned up through doing the Eight Brocades.

The sitting Eight Brocades is much more meditative and focused on establishing inner rhythms with much more subtle movements, though some variations of the sitting Eight Brocades contain similar aspects to the standing series.

9. Massage yourself and others. All the various forms of massage, tai chi, chi gung, yoga, most exercise and all various bodywork all share the basic quality of relaxation through opening and expanding the body. As children we start off as soft and malleable dreamers. As the world turns we face turmoil, if only occasionally, which can result in fear or injury which can result in clenching and tightening. These healing practices remove the fears and pains, allowing ourselves to open up, create movement and become balanced. Movement results in balance which begins healing and when we are healed we can dream again.

There are 108 main pressure points in acupressure and in martial arts, though of the specific points mentioned some occasionally differ. There are said to be 36 primary points and 72 secondary points. In acupuncture there are 361 main points and many other lesser points. Massaging these points can elevate wellbeing and alleviate unease. One of the most important acupressure points is called stomach 36. This point is located along the tibia, just to the outside of the shin about a hand length down from the knee. You will know it when you find it. Massaging this point leads to better digestion and increased vitality.

Rub the soles of your feet 81 times -or more- with the knife edge of you hand, once, twice or three times a day. 81 times is the minimum one should rub one's soles, 81 being three fourths of 108 and containing the 1 and the 8. Rubbing the soles 108 times is definitely just as good and possibly better than 81 times, as I was taught 81 times is the minimum number one should do to attain benefits. In Chinese medicine the soles of the feet are called the bubbling spring and they reflect the rest of bodies. This chi gung massage is said to alone yield to good health and longevity all by itself. I can't emphasize the importance of this massage enough. Stretch your toes and massage variously after intense rubbing as well.

Tai chi, chi gung and yoga (all traceable back to Hindu dance and meditative movements) are ancient and yet they have roots in more primordial practices. Before the internal arts and martial arts there was bone tapping. Bone tapping is a vigorous and stimulating self-massage basically. Bone tapping is an excellent to warm up before any practice or day. This series works upward. Tap you shins and the muscle on the side of the shins with your knuckles or a stick up to 27 or 36 times. Most all simple practices in tai chi and chi gung are done in repetitions divisible by 3, and 9. Tap the back of your knees and the back of your legs solidly with your palms or any part of your fist 6 to 12 times. Tap or pat your upper thighs and then your inner thighs. Use the back of your hand to tap your lower back, your sacrum and tailbone as many times as you like. Tap you your kidneys in the same way only more gently 6 to 12 times. Tap the top of your shoulders and slide down your arms with your palm 6 to 36 times. Rub your belly and pat your abdomen and chest. Tap the back of your shoulders the same way. Remember to apply the same strength and tap each side the same number of times. Lightly tap your jaw. Pull your ear lobes. Lightly tap all over the back over the neck and head, then tap the crown of your head with you knuckles a little harder. Lastly tap your collarbones being mindful of their sensitivity as the most fragile bones of the body.

Rubbing can be utilized with or on top of bone tapping as well. You can rub your shins with the heel of your hands from the knee downward to expel blocked energy. When rubbing your belly, chest and back do equal circles, in each direction, ideally with each hand, each way or both hands at the same time each way. Gently rub your neck from below your chin to your sternum. With your middle finger rub the sides of the nose, under the eyes around six times. Rub your forehead side to side and with the other hand rub your face side to side, then switch hands. Then switch to rub each side up and down. Gently rub your face, side to side, up and down, alternating, direction and hands.

Tibetan yoga practitioners will sit in lotus position with their legs locked and lift themselves up with their hands and drop onto the tailbone and buttocks remaining in the full lotus. This is a highly stimulating practice, physically and energetically. One can also simply hop up and down from this position to tap his area.

Some Tibetan yogis practice variations of hopping up from lotus position and then, in midair, returning to lotus position as they fall back to the ground, an extremely complicated maneuver during which you could easily break your leg. Do not attempt.

Stand about a foot or less, whatever feels comfortable, from a solid wall and allow yourself to fall back onto it. Exhale out as you allow your back to tap the wall. Allow yourself to variously gently fall onto your shoulders, upper back and lower back. This process stimulates and generates chi.

The power of a simple hug or just touching someone positively can be powerful and remain powerful for a time in diffusing anger and sadness. An embrace or pat on the back can infuse love and happiness and it cannot be underestimated. A simple hug can change everything. Embrace so that your hearts touch. Rub and/or pat their back. Hug and give mutual massages so that you know what feels good and where. Our skin is the only organ we can touch and it is important to massage, tap, rub, flick at, pull on and hit too stimulate movement for movement leads to balance.

A bruise is merely unmoved blood, and potentially chi, which is stagnant and blocked. Extrapolated and enhanced on, many illnesses result from similar blockages. If you experience a painful impact or twist keep it warm by applying hot towels or otherwise applying heat for the first 24 hours or so and be sure to rub, pat, tap and move circularly to maintain what is decreased blood flow. After keeping it warm or hot for the first 24 hours apply twenty minutes of heat and twenty minutes of ice repeatedly. The more you apply intense heat and intense cold the faster you will heal. If you concentrate on this application of temperature change you will surprise yourself as to how fast you heal. Ice slows blood flow and heat increases it, moving and displacing the clogged blood causing bruising. Such contraction and expansion whether through temperature change or tension change or alternation of exertive and relaxed meditative movements can be highly effective for healing and strengthening.

10. Smile inwardly and outwardly. Emotions are like bodies of water. Some are more easily stirred than others. Try to be steady. A smile inwardly can change your day and a smile outwardly can change everyone's day. A smile can instigate friendship and distinguish confrontation. A smile can create steady, calm and serene seas.

There is a centuries old Taoist meditation called the Inner Smile in which one smiles inwardly to the whole body beginning at the crown of the head. The process takes twenty to thirty minutes at first. Sit on the edge of a chair with your hands on your knees like an Egyptian or sit cross legged on the floor. Smile softly. Breathe slowly through your nose. Imagine your breathing from and to your heart. Imagine loving light, compassion, focus and relaxation gathering in your mind. Imagine the light and smile infused energy resonating to ever cell of your body. Smile to every part of your body specifically beginning with you're the crown of your head the eyes, face and jaw. Then imagine lightening up any blockages or pains down through your throat, thymus and thyroid. Imagine the light removing tension in all the muscles and organs from your heart, lungs, down to your liver and kidneys. Imagine the energy lighting up your spine and each vertebrae. And eventually imagine light gathering in the dantien, below the navel. Consciousness as well as the universal energy of chi or prana must first be imagined using the power of the mind and then, as your practice unfolds, imagination is no longer required. Imagination is initially needed for activation of chi and then the energy just is.

11. Learn how to lift weights using tai chi principles of slow, steady, relaxed intensity. Never exceed more than ~80% exertion in training upper body, and ~60% when training your legs. Never lock or bring your elbows or knees or any joints to extended straight positioning. Increase repetition before increasing weight. Aim for sets of between 9 or 15 with the upper body and between 20 or 40 with lower body, light weight and higher the repetitions done slowly is best.

One does not need a gym to workout. Hiking and biking are excellent for health and fun. Weights can be made from buckets. Curls and shoulder shrugs can be done easily using buckets. Different pushups, sit-ups, dips, wall-ups and pull-ups can all be done without a gym. Try pushups on your palms wide and narrow positioning, try on your fingertips eventually. Do pull-ups wide and narrow palms facing away from you and do narrow with palms facing you. Do them with one hand facing each way and alternate.

Weight and resistance training can benefit everyone, in fact muscle strength might be more important than aerobic strength. Remember to better form before adding weight and keep your back straight. Exercise does not require exhaustion. Take it slow.

Try employing prostrations, a relaxing and invigorating metaphysical exercise. Begin standing with your feet together. Bring your hands together in prayer and raise them to the crown of your head, then down to your, forehead, throat and heart. And continue down to press the palms to floor, then to your knees, then step your hands forward so your hands, lie down and reach out about above you as you rest your chest and forehead to the floor while remaining on your toes. The feet stay in more or less the same position. Prostrations are a great way to heal. Try to reach the point where you can do 21 repetitions. Many Buddhist monks will commit to doing 108,000 prostrations across great distances as part of a way to be open and humbly compassionate.

Think about employing plyometric and isometric workouts as opposed to traditional dynamic exercises. Isometrics involves holding a prone position until your muscles fire out. Stand on one foot for a length of time and on the other for an equal time period. Hold light weights, water bottles can be used, prone until your muscles tire. Try holding your arms in front of you, above your head variously and to the sides.

Many chi gung positions hold static meditative standing positions. In fact one way to feel chi is to stand perfectly still with your feet about shoulder width, knees unlocked. Your hands can be at your sides or just in front of your waist. Imagine there are energy balls in between your legs, behind you, under your arms and that you're holding a ball to reinforce relaxed and unlocked positioning. This is often called bell posture. Try meditating in bell posture until one experiences spontaneous movement. The spontaneous movement is akin to, but often slightly different from random muscle firing.

Plyometric work outs involve short, fast bursts of intense, explosive energy output. Jump up to position six inches to two feet or higher and back down. Always start small and work your way up with any routine.

You can adopt one of the simple and physically brutal Shaolin monk exercises. Part of Shaolin training is running upstairs to the top of their sacred mountain and then walking down the same set of stairs on their palms and toes without touching their elbows or knees. Combining running upstairs and walking down them on all fours will develop enormous strength and vitality.

12. Walk or run in natural settings. Walk barefoot in clean environments to initiate electrical and chi contact with the Earth. Simply walking barefoot on nourished and conductive ground can instigate healing and attune oneself with your surroundings. Walk on the balls of your feet or the tips of your toes. Imagine you weigh one ton and walk slowly sinking your energy. Imagine each step sinks deep into the earth. If you have bad posture, begin to adjust yourself by walking like a pigeon: point your toes inward as you go, stepping on your toes or heels first. Do not walk and do not stand like a duck or a like clown. When standing put your weight primarily on one foot pointed straight ahead, the other can be pointed outward no more than 45 degrees.

A simple thing like improper posture while standing and walking can lead to long term discomfort. When we are mindful of our feet we are mindful of our entire body and can adjust our posture and alignment.

Tai chi walking, the crawl or brush knee push step, adopts part of the tai chi long form and repeats it. Step forward with your left foot, heel touching the ground first. The step should be or at least should thought of a round sweeping movement. With your right hand imagine pushing someone's sternum with your palm and/or releasing energy through the palms and fingers. Then repeat with the right leg forward and left palm pushing from near the shoulder. Move slowly and in coordination with the breath. Try walking backwards doing the same thing pushing with the right as you step back with the left. The left right dynamic increases your awareness and heightens brain activity. Walking backwards in this way is called repulse the monkey.

To further increase your leg strength do squats without any weight. The slower you move the more muscular exertion you create. Do not let your toes go past your knees, keep your toes straight and pretend to sit down and rise up extremely slowly. Do tai chi squats. Beginning from the lotus position on a soft floor, twist and stand keeping your feet in place turning a full 360 and then squat back down turning 0. When you repeat it next you will end up alternating the direction you flow up and down. Adjust your feet as needed, a slightly more narrow positioning can be helpful and use your hands initially if needed. Ultimately meditative performance of these squats with the breath inhaling up and exhaling down, combined with meditation in lotus makes this one position a serious energy builder by itself.

Much of the natural world has been paved over. Running, jogging and even walking on concrete can physically rattle our legs and metaphysically insulates us, preventing us from earth connection as do our rubber soled shoes. When on concrete, walk lightly. When you're running or jogging, if at all possible make sure to be on earthen ground or simply hike where you can be on earthen ground. And take your shoes off when you are able.

Pa Qua circle walking is a wonderful martial and meditative art that is extremely energizing. There are several forms of this type of kung fu, the simplest parts of which concentrate on meditatively walking in a circle. Beginner practitioners walk in a circle utilizing different hand positions and spinning changes. Set something on the floor for reference and walk around it so that the circumference is about eight steps, though any size will work. Concentrate on how you are walking rather than your hand positioning. The lower, longer and slower your steps are the more of a physical workout circle walking will be. Be mindful of your steps. Sliding the stepping foot on the floor as you go is a variation that sets your footing correctly. Always keep your knees above your feet, never linearly beyond your toes.

Walking the square is another variation of pa qua circle walking. Simply walk in a small circle, or square. Place your heel adjacently to your other toe at 180 degree rotations so that you walk a full rotation every four steps. Keep your knees unlocked and step lightly. Do walking meditations barefoot. All meditative traditions speak of ground to the earth and several scientific systems suggest we literally do electrically ground to the earth.

13. Change your mind. Whenever we experience ascension or betterment we realize it and so do others. Whether meditating on compassion in equanimity or learning something which elevates and raises one's sense of being, when one rises upwards and it sometimes seems that one's peers want to hold you back and hold you down from ascension. Meditation changes your mind and changes everything around you, and people sometimes have negative reactions to the spiritual movement and might do something uncalled for, perhaps unconsciously reacting to your ascension, to your mind

changing. Their reactions can seem very much like someone jumping onto your rising consciousness to hold you down in base conundrums, but in actuality they are jumping on so they can ascend too. It feels like peers may be dragging you down when you concurrently feel you are rising up, but it's simply they don't know how to do it themselves, they aren't dragging you down, but metaphysically trying to catch a ride upward and ascend with you, but because of the gross plane we exist in, everything is misinterpreted and misunderstood. Change your mind, for it can change the situation entirely.

14. Stretch and play. There are numerous forms of stretching and different ways of doing the same stretches. The best stretches are often the simplest and those done in a playful manner. When stretching think of opening up, but don't think of it as stretching and certainly don't force it, just be. Be mindful never to go to the point of extreme exertion and don't lock the joints. If it hurts don't do it.

Kneel on your knees and shins with one big toe crossing on top of the other. Hold this position and relax.

Sit with your legs in front of you. Set one foot on top of the other thigh, to form a bow. Alternate, repeat.

Sit with your legs in front of you and reach for your toes. Hold your feet from the top of the toes or ankles or shins, depending on your flexibility. Instead of bringing your head to your feet, in this stretch think about putting your head down to the floor between your knees. Then change the position. Shift your back so you're looking straight ahead and your back is not curved, but straight and aligned. Hold this position. This is one of the most complicated, contemplated and debated stretches.

Stand and reach above you, then bend forward and down to touch or hold your toes, head toward being in between the knees.

Stand with your feet well beyond shoulder width, toes pointed out straight, reach up and to the right with your left arm while pressing below the right knee on the side of your leg with your right hand and alternate.

Place your legs about three or more feet apart and bend forward to the floor. Walk yourself forward with your hands so that your back is straight and aligned, then as comfortable elongate a little more and when ready walk back.

Place a walking stick or broomstick or similar a couple of feet in front of you so that you can grab it and bend forward. Adjust your back and neck so they are aligned and nearly perfectly straight. Adjust the height of your hand position and the placement of the walking stick as needed. Hold the position as long as you like. Stretch to the point of feeling opening and release, but do not cause yourself pain. Think of stretching as just being, not forcing a movement.

Whatever it is you do that makes you smile or laugh or become excited to compete or be athletic; do it. We can be in The Zone doing anything, but there are few opportunities to be there as easily as playing where we can shed the distractions otherwise hindering. And whether it is the intuitive recognition of your teammate's eye movement or understanding of the conditions ahead as you're sliding downhill, being in The Zone is a valuable wherever it occurs. Try to play a game like basketball without using your voice and see if you can communicate and coordinate non-vocally. Playing is whatever activity that you think about doing when you're doing other things, and the thing that when you're doing, you don't think about anything else.

One overlooked activity which can develop your left and right side integration as well as better your lower body balance is using a hackey sack. It develops concentration and the ability to finely touch with your feet which helps in learning meditative movement where arms and legs move in unison with the breath.

15. Move. Do not sit, stand, walk or lie down for too long. Stagnancy and redundant repetition of any sort will potentially rot you. Don't be stagnant for movement leads to balance and good health. However occasionally practice being completely still. Practice standing, walking, lying and sitting meditation while being physically still. Stand perfectly still for a minute or longer and try to ground or root yourself. Sit completely still on your chair or in cross legged position. Lie down flat on your back completely still. Walk slowly so that your upper body above your torso is still, in line with the hips. Stillness is meditative, however meditation is not stagnancy. In meditation the physical

is still and we attempt to still the mind, but the consciousness is active during meditation and inactive during stagnant stillness.

"Sleep is unconscious meditation. Mediation is conscious sleep." ~Unknown

16. Learn and practice tai chi rocking, a meditative balance exercise. Begin by standing with feet about shoulder width apart. On the inhalation bring your hands, palms facing up, just in front of you and lift your heels slightly and to put your weight on your toes. On the exhalation rotate your hands so that your palms are facing downward at first as if clawing in front of you and then bring them behind you lifting your toes and putting all your weight on your heels. That's inhale palms up, as if serving tea and exhale clawing down, like a cat. Repeat for five, ten or more minutes. Practice lifting the feet slowly for a moment or two. Practice rocking your feet just barely and briefly lifting, but completely teetering on edge. Practice keeping your feet rooted, but going to the subtle tipping point. It's ok to lose your balance and reposition, in fact it means you were teetering. Practice with your eyes closed. Imagine the movement coming from your lower belly, your dantien.

Later you can vary this movement. Perform the opposite movement with your hands; when you are on your toes bring them just behind you and when you are on your heels bring them in front of you. You can vary the breathing as well, though the first form is the best. Never put your knees past your toes.

This movement physically fires off micro muscles that normally would not be activated, increasing your muscle firing speed later on. Energetically this movement enhances flow by relaxing the mind's chatter in creating movement of the hands, feet and dantien in unison with the breath. Such meditative movement, upper and lower body breath coordinated movement gives the mind something to be present on.

17. Eat quality food. Eat fruits and berries. The root word of the word vaccination is berry. Humans and fruit bats are the only mammals that do not produce our own vitamin C. Eat fruits and especially berries for health. Eat garlic. If you feel yourself becoming sick eat more garlic. It is one of the best ways to detoxify, prevent sickness and assists in ridding oneself of the cold and flu. Eat greens like chlorella, spinach,

spirulina, kale, cilantro, darker lettuce, broccoli and wheatgrass. Eat roots like ginseng, ginger, turmeric, astragalus and maca root. Eat cacao and dark chocolate.

Eat immune boosting cancer preventatives now. Apple cider vinegar, wine, turmeric, ginger, non-GMO vitamin C, vitamin D, coffee, tea, mushrooms (cordyceps, reishi, shitake, lion's tail, maitake, mushroom extracts are enormously effective in assisting combating all illnesses.) honey, bee pollen, propolis/royal jelly, apricot seeds, cinnamon, pomegranate, cherry, cranberry, soursop, ginseng, ginger. Apricots and almonds eaten together are legendary for their therapeutic qualities.

18. Avoid toxins. Do not eat potato chips. Many substances nontoxic substances can be transformed into toxic substances by application of temperature changes. When potatoes are fried in oil a chemical change occurs resulting in toxins. You can feel the toxins in your belly if you eat a lot of chips. Some substances are entirely toxin without any chemical change. Most cleaners are horrible for the environment and you. Try castile soap, citrus cleaners, vinegar, plant sourced soaps and water. Boiling hot water is an amazing cleaner.

Do not use chemical sunblock. It contains toxins, poisons you and the environment. Wear a hat, or cover up more. Sesame seed oil, avocado oil, peanut oil, coconut oil, Shea butter, wheat germ oil, carrot oil and hemp oil are all alternatives.

Avoid dairy products. Dairy feeds growing cancers as it does growing mammals. So if you are not a baby mammal, don't consume milk or dairy products. Avoid wheat. Avoid refined sugar.

Don't use a microwave and forego franchise fast food. The microwave reflects the short cut society that would rather have fast, cheap food rather than fresh, nutritious food, food that looks good rather than being good. The microwave oven cooks food from the inside out through radiation. It destroys enzymes and perhaps alters the food. Franchise fast food is rarely fresh and barely bears fruit toward development or maintenance of the health and wellbeing of those who eat the food or those who work for the franchise.

Microwaves, cellphones and wireless computers all emit powerful energy. The electromagnetic pollution resulting from cellphones and cellphone towers can be extremely harmful. Studies indicate that simply carrying cellular devices can increase the likelihood of developing tumors in the area where the device is carried. The electromagnetic power and disturbance directly near the devices are thousands of times more intense than just a foot away. Constant use of cellular devices may increase the likelihood of cancer. Do not eat hydrogenated oil, genetically modified foods, aspartame or anything else you cannot create in your home kitchen. Most corn, wheat and soy grown in the U.S.A. are all genetically modified organisms designed in a laboratory to grow utilizing petrochemical toxins which kill all other plants, insects and animals which come in contact with it in the field. Many tomatoes and papayas are GMO. Sugar, if not implicitly stated as cane sugar, is most likely derived from beet sugar, processed from GMO beets. Generally speaking one should avoid vitamin supplements which are not plant sourced and most vitamins contain GMOs. Eat natural, eat simple and go organic.

19. Be the one. Humanity is a funny bunch. The less conscious people are the more likely they are to mock and confront those with perceived differences in appearance and class especially. There is individual and mass consciousness evident in the behavior differences of friends when they are with you or with certain groups of others. People will behave less consciously when in certain groups. If you are the one, you set the tone of the group or at least don't let the tone of the group set you.

Wear a funny hat. Be different. Don't go so far as to get yourself hurt. That is, if your society won't tolerate your hat, wear a different shoelace so to speak. Be the one that everyone laughs at. See if they look you in the eyes when they are doing so. Then take off the hat. Be on the side that they predominant ostracize and act like one and then show the predominant how wrong they were for making assumptions that the funny hat was you.

Be the one to raise your hand and ask the question. Be the one to lend a hand for assistance. Be the one to grab the hand of someone acting violently. Be the one to say demonstratively, no or yes, whatever happens to be contrarian to the swayed mass consciousness. Be the one that they laugh at and look to in awe. Make sure you look people in the eye when doing so. See if they can look at you back.

All the great consciousness is ridiculed and lunged upon and then they fight back. In one way or another all great consciousness fights back literally or figuratively. This is philosophically represented in Hegel's Master Slave Dialectic, the story of Jesus, the story of Buddha, the story of Moses and a million other stories of people standing up for themselves and becoming. Always be the one to shake off people riding the backs of mass consciousness. You will be ridiculed and you will be respected as the one always is.

Be yourself and put forth your vision. Find a hero to identify with as a role model, besides those in contemporary circles that you can aspire to be like in how they stood up among their contemporaries, as themselves. All heroes always break away from the contemporary crowd. Jesus was loved by all –individuals and was hated by all the institutions of his day, because he was himself and put forth his own vision. Be like Noah. He built his ark and as he built his dream everyone made fun of him. But everybody wanted a ride in the end. Be like Ganesh. Ganesh, the elephant headed Hindu god, the god of writers, is also known as the obstacle breaker or in contrast, the obstacle maker.

20. Keep it simple. The most simple concepts and acts are the most powerful and effective when well thought out and well put. Consider the Pareto Principle, the 80 20 rule, or law of the vital few. The idea states that essentially 80% of results arise from 20% causes. The idea originated in Pareto's garden. He found that 80% of his peas were from 20% of the pods. The Pareto Principle is often applied to economics, but can be applied to multiple systems, such as 80% of your nutrition is obtained from 20% of your consumption or 80% of the benefits of exercise result from 20% of your efforts. The specifics vary, but most often this ratio can be extrapolated. The more complexity one includes the worse the ratio tends to become. By enhancing simplicity, by keeping one's operations simple one is more likely to approach better results and ratios.

Eat only until you are about 80% - 85% full. Never overeat. The Warrior Diet prepares one for anything and is considered optimal for marching all day and still being prepared with energy for serious exertion in battle. The warrior eats small amounts frequently, so as to always have energy, but not be tired from digestion.

21. Learn and practice tai chi push hands. This exercise, done with a partner can greatly increase balance and be a fun cooperative challenge and energy builder for those of all

ages and athletic abilities. As with practically all tai chi and chi gung stances imagine there are lines extending from under your feet and make it so the lines do not intersect at the feet. Tai chi theory tends to follow what is physically and even metaphysically, the optimal.

There are numerous ways to do push hands the simplest is standing still and with partners facing each in mirror image one foot in front of the other one foot points straight ahead and the other foot, at about shoulder width, or more has toes pointed out at approximately 45 degrees. The lead wrist or forearm meets and engages the mutual body part of partner. The lead arm generally engages more actively and the other more passively. The amount of force exchanged is mutually accepted and felt out, gently. Push hands is not sparring though some martial artists that spar practice it too. The exchange can be gentle or forceful and builds chi the same, but only through being gentle will sensitivity develop. The point is to relax and increase sensitivity, not spar. There can be many variations to the pressure involved, the speed, the stance and the rate of pushing and yielding. The rotational engagement off the hands revolves much like the shape of the Yin Yang symbol. Keep your feet rooted. Don't forget to switch sides for balance.

The idea is to always be touching and even when you're not touching physically, to be in touch intuitively. Push hands is optimally practiced in gentle terms so as to build this intuitive sense, with the intention of gently pushing your partner off balance so that each practitioner learns better balance. Optimal push hands technique doesn't exert force, as much as it utilizes force, in doing so one easily moves tremendous energy. This reflects the tai chi idea that the force of four ounces moves one thousand pounds; direct focused energy is appropriate not brutish force, in push hands and life.

22. Know where your food is from. Green tea is one of the best things to drink and yet tea from Japan and Fukushima Prefecture in particular definitely has radiological contamination. Fish once might have been a delicious source of valuable fat and protein however today they might be contaminated as well whether from Japan, the Pacific Ocean or Mediterranean Sea, or, I am sorry to say, practically everywhere. The West Coast of North America is set to be the hardest hit by the Fukushima fallout outside of Japan. In pursuing capitalistic ends we have ignored all other measurements of prosperity and now the Pacific Ocean is a nuclear fuel pool and Japan is sinking.

Some of the best ways to mitigate radiation are natural. Alcohol proved to assist removal of radiation in Chernobyl in the short term. Iodine can protect the thyroid from absorbing radioactive iodine. Generally speaking, supplying the body with all the nutrients it needs helps mitigate the effects of exposure and eliminates the likelihood the body will absorb the radioactive metals it mistakes for nutritious minerals. The problem with radioactive elements is that the body absorbs them in many different ways as we do different elements. Apple pectin absorbs radiation. Lemon balm and ginger mitigate the effects of radiation. Miso soup and all probiotics assist the body in ridding radiation too. Coffee and more specifically the boron in it absorbs radiation. Turmeric helps remove radiation and is wonderful for overall health. All freshwater and salt water algae like chlorella, spirulina and blue green algae can work wonders, as well as green tea, garlic, resveratrol, sulfur, calcium, vitamin C, zeolite and boron. Some research suggests marijuana ingestion repairs DNA damage, potentially including DNA damage from radiation.

23. If you drink alcohol, don't do so excessively or frequently. Go with the high end alcohol as it tends to have less toxins. Try wine or an herbal extract of sorts. Most beer today contains direct genetically modified ingredients. Much of the accompaniments to alcohol convert to sugars in the body, which do not assist in maintaining longevity, but do result in hangovers. Single malt Scotch has few hangover causing chemicals.

Alcohol should be limitedly consumed, if at all. At least do not drink large quantities and do not drink frequently unless it is one drink a day, but even still one can't meditate drunk. Drinking can lead to troubled sleep for many people, troubled health for everyone and occasional reckless troubles for those who drink too much. Drinking alcohol causes ill health, ill behavior and premature aging. However drinking can be medicinal. Alcohol kills germs of course, and it was found that the Chernobyl soldiers who drank more alcohol absorbed less of the radioactive elements around the plant.

At one point there were noted to be 108 elements on the chart of elements. Today there are considered to be 118 known elements charted into 18 related columns, 99 of which have been found naturally on Earth, the rest only synthesized or claimed to have been synthesized.

24. Learn and practice at least one type of yoga Sun Salutation. A Sun Salutation is a series of yoga postures repeated in homage to the sun inside us and the sun we orbit around. These are traditionally done in the morning facing the rising Sun. Some yoga practitioners perform 108 sun salutations on the winter and summer solstices in homage to the metaphysical microcosmic and macrocosmic correlation. This process takes about two hours. Two similar Sun Salutations are illustrated below, the simpler form in the middle circle.

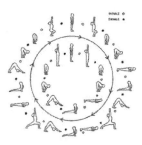

According to well established tai chi, chi gung and some yoga the optimal time to practice is during sunset or sunrise, the hour after sunrise and the hour before sunset. Other times have their specific benefits, but sunrise and sunset are optimal in order to gain energy from the Sun. During these time periods we are compelled to look at the Sun, to watch it, when meditating or not. Ancient traditions suggest people can obtain energy from the Sun during these periods just by being in its light as well as looking into it. The practice is called sun eating and one is supposed to start with ten seconds and work your way up to forty minutes or so via up five to ten second intervals in order to gain solar energy.

Practically all life is dependent on the light emitted from the sun. Recent studies reveal that not only does life absorb light, but plants and animals emit light as well. Healthy human beings emit light, we have auras and radiate biophotons, ultraweak emissions of light. These biophoton emissions can be directed onto the outside world. We absorb and emit light and we can direct the emissions for healing among other things. Research found that herbs and meditation slowed the rate of light emission. Further research found that our intention can manifest and provoke changes to the outside world through the emission of biophotons. Science and spirituality conclude we are dependent on, made up of and emit light. These biophoton emissions can be focused so as to heal animate being and manipulate inanimate objects.

25. Break addictions. Sometimes the best way to break an addiction is to replace it with a new activity, even before one completely stops the old activity. Sometimes the replacement activity for a negative addiction might be the opposite type of activity. If you are trying to cease being a smoker, become a runner. If you are trying to cease eating chemically processed meats and genetically modified organisms, start eating organic fruits and nuts. Eventually you will find the old activity is not distasteful. Sometimes the chemical addiction is so overwhelming that one must find an alternative chemical as a replacement.

Buddhists believe that actions result in karma in this life, whereas thoughts result in karma for next life. George Orwell said, 'At age fifty, everyman has the face he deserves.' Nothing will give you such a haggard expression, nothing will remove your smile and leave scarring regret where there was open optimism quicker than an addiction. Nothing will rot your core so completely from the inside out as an addiction, alcoholism being one of the worst among them. The ancients all had religious or national celebrations where they would get twisted –about once a year! Do not spend your life as an alcoholic or meth addict when there are so many other things you could do. Do not end up a fifty year old alcoholic or meth addict, or forty, or twenty or any other age.

Marijuana can be used as a non-addictive and relatively harmless alternative to break other chemical addictions. If you suffer from anxiety try marijuana. It is probably the safest drug in existence and can be relaxing in a stressful world. If you seek intoxication, there is no other drug needed beyond marijuana. Practically all other drugs under practically any circumstances are dangerous and detrimental, including alcohol. All smoke is potentially carcinogenic, however marijuana and hemp have many healing properties, even the smoke of marijuana.

Marijuana is not addictive though it can be abused. If you find yourself abusing marijuana or if marijuana is not a suitable replacement for your nonchemical addiction or abusive behavior try meditation. Meditation can bring about states of bliss and happiness which chemicals occasionally replicate.

26. Stop buying drinks in plastic containers and cease using plastic containers as much as possible. Temperature change, hot and cold, can cause toxins in the plastic to leak into the fluid. Sometimes you cannot avoid it nowadays. However one can carry glass jars and glass bottles of water when feasible. Doing so reduces the burden of plastic toxicity on you and on the environment.

Try to reduce consumption of canned sodas and other similar drinks as all sugary concoctions lead to debilitating diseases as do many of the elements the container is lined with. Try to minimize eating any canned goods too as the foods are tainted with container chemicals, it's not as nutritious as fresh food and reducing waste is good for the environment. Why glass jars are not utilized so poisonous chemicals are not used is revelatory of corporate measure of profit above all else, including the health of the consumer. Carry a cup with you if at all possible. The single serving society results in over consumption and unnecessary pollution and corporate control. Plastic bags kill life on Earth through the toxins released and in being unleashed as litter for everything from birds to whales to unknowingly consume.

27. Travel and be adventurous, adaptable and altruistic as you go. Go outside the country or down the street, but travel outside your normal social circles and immerse yourself in the world -by yourself. You will never know who you are until you can see yourself, by yourself in a world outside your cultural comfort zone. You will learn about yourself as an individual and you will learn about us all, as a collective. Adversity, such as the adversity of simply being a lone outsider, whether in a different neighborhood or different country, builds character and character garners support. You will become more comfortable in more places, with more people.

28. Seek silence from mass consciousness and your own conscious thinking. Seek moments of complete silence alone, if only occasionally, if only for a moment. Try to experience total silence and total darkness occasionally. We think so much about the past, present and pretend that seeking moments of inner quiet is totally necessary - even if impossible. Even if one is unable to relax and think of nothing but breath, trying

itself is soothing –eventually. Try counting the breaths to take your mind away from chattering disgusting thinking. See how high you can count before being distracted.

Try doing things (safely) with a blindfold on or earplugs in to develop your other senses, restricting the senses strengthens them all. Try to silence the chatter of the mind so you can truly think. Whether in meditation or just in nature silence heals and enlightens. Do not have imaginary confrontations and illusions steer you. We are astute thinkers, but we also can fall into the trappings of our active ego. The ego will bring about imaginary delusions and influence one to act on preconceptions. Quiet yourself always. Try not to have imaginary conversations and confrontations. "Be newborn, be free of yourself." ~Lao Tzu

The five senses are often considered five needs, five ways in which we need fulfillment in one way or another. Our senses are like insistent children, constantly in need of input. Turning off the needs of the five senses allows us to go inside and reach the sixth sense, the intuitive potential of our consciousness.

29. Greet and acknowledge acquaintances in crowds and strangers in the open alone. Be honest and at the same time practice empathy. Learn and use tact and grace in relationships. Think of teaching or leading by example. Be open to discussion and advice. As difficult of a process as it may be, first must come the truth, like earth envelopes the seed, before trust will bloom. Whether you want to be liked, want to be kind or want to be a leader, follow these steps and people will appreciate and even follow you.

30. Try to exalt the people you speak with. The more you uplift those around you the more you are uplifted, the more kind you are the more kind people will be. If someone informs you of themselves try not to flip it into a way that could benefit you. If someone tells you that they write, do not respond that you are open for interviews.

If you cannot speak kind words at least make sure that what you say about them, you also say to them. No one likes someone who is constantly badmouthing others. And at the same time, never be a sycophant. Even the person you are kissing up to will not like you or respect you for it. Be exceptionally nice to all, equally. Be straight and direct and honest, people will respect you for it, but don't insert hollow kindness to set yourself up in some way.

31. Never mistake kindness for weakness. Ultimately on top of increasing friction, you will never be treated well. Be aware that many people are shallow and as you expand and grow deeper, shallow people will identify with you less. Shallow people will be exceptionally friendly with you if you have something to offer them and real people who are real friends will approach you friendly always. So never mistake kindness for weakness, but also be wary of kindness as a way to finesse. True kindness is imparted on those who you will get nothing in return.

Be compassionate and don't hate. The best way to impact the people around you and the planet and leave your mark in a positive manner is to help people without expecting return or benefit. The best way to keep you energy is to not let others get you angry unnecessarily. Never spend time thinking about what others should do, or worse contemplating how to get revenge, even in the slightest social fashion, for it depletes you of your energy which could be used to balance and better you.

32. Be aware of the transmutational potential of everything. The only constant is change. Water is present in liquid, solid and vapor. Liquid water turns to solid ice at 32 degrees Fahrenheit. The water then expands to around 108% of its original volume. The vaporization temperature of water depends on the barometric pressure it is under, for instance at sea level water turns to steam at about 100 degrees and atop Mount Everest at 154 degrees, while water in the pressurized depths of the oceans remains liquid near geothermal vents at hundreds of degrees Fahrenheit.

We are made up of mostly water and our functions depend on clean water, like car batteries need distilled water. Water is affected by its environment, it absorbs everything as the ultimate solvent and so do we, being mostly water. This is true physically as water absorbs, filters and redistributes the traceable poisons man has emitted into the environment as do we. On a deeper water absorbs, is affected by and carries emotions. Positive emotions, positive vibrations lead to balanced geometrically symmetrical water droplets, like beautiful snowflakes each different and perfect, while negative emotions and words can transform beauty into deformity.

The practitioners of the ancient art of alchemy are most legendary for seeking the mineral transmutation of lead into gold. However this secret process was used to institute concealment and distraction from another alchemical transmutation secret. The real secret of alchemical transmutation is not only mineral, but biological. Alchemists sought to rejuvenate life, alchemists sought immortality, bettered and extended being. Alchemists sought to be golden, the only mineral which doesn't oxidize. Further they wanted to develop their minds from having dull lead like thoughts into having golden thoughts. And they wanted to transform their physical the same.

Whether it is time, pressure, temperature, altitude or another natural factor outside of our personal microcosm affecting us like conditions affect water or a thought, something we develop inside ourselves we are capable of transmutation into golden being or lead like being. Train or be trained. Be like pristine water. Think of 108 and your life. Think about how you can go from one thing, to nothing, to anything.

Remember that at one time you knew nothing of certain concepts you know now and had only a fraction of the maturity that you had now. Remember that others are in their own process of development and transmutation. We all need help to evolve, otherwise we can devolve.

33. Reach for perfection. Take on things which might be more complicated than you are prepared for and attempt to hone and perfect the image, the phrase or the movement or whatever it is you are doing. Then reduce the complexity and see how refined you have become. Practice things slowly and thoughtfully.

Reach for perfection with a gentle blissful understanding that we are mortal and though you may get a perfect 10 we are all flawed and as so can only improve by reaching higher. We can only at best reach for perfection and we must in order to attain greatness.

Only try your first time. Every other time do. Do. Do not try. The universal energy lends beginners luck to true neophytes and true hearty tries can often be enough your first time, but after that you must make it happen. Thinking about trying leads one to trying, whereas thinking about doing makes it done.

34. Learn. If you ever think you know enough, you've failed. There are two models of understanding the learning process which can help one learn and stay motivated to learn and teach. The inventor and philosopher Arthur Young proposed four steps to initiating learning. First there is unconscious action such as reaching out to fire, then unconscious reaction, pulling away from the heat. Next is conscious reaction, such as avoiding fire in the future and lastly is conscious action, utilization of fire without being hurt.

The Conscious Competence psychological model goes beyond mere learning into the idea of mastery. The first stage is unconscious incompetence, being ignorant of ignorance. The second stage is conscious incompetence, realizing one's ignorance. Thirdly is conscious competence, being capable. And finally is unconscious competence, mastery. One goes from ignorance, to realization of ignorance, to capably skilled and ultimately one can do it in your sleep. Unconscious competence is being in the Zone.

Arthur Young, a philosopher and inventor, also theorized a fourfold learning process. First there is unconscious action as if reaching for fire, then unconscious reaction as if feeling its heat and pulling away. This is followed by unconscious reaction in the future to avoid being burned. Ultimately the fourth stage is conscious action, the utilization and mastery of fire as tool. Learning itself is a four stage transformational process based on the matrix of four and the philosophy of the duality of polarity. Keep learning, keep thinking and one can transform unconscious action, of which you are unaware of into conscious action.

Do not be afraid to make mistakes when learning new things. However always weigh the risk/reward ratio. Compare what might be gained, with what is at risk and the likelihood of what is at risk happening. Slow and steady progression is better than hyper spurts of learning punctuated by periods stagnated by injuries. Fools rush in lacking conscious mastery.

35. Learn about consciousness. And expand yours. A primary presentation of consciousness is articulated in the Om symbol. Throughout the day we exist in the wake state and dream state being awake or asleep. The third state is known as deep sleep. This state is the Zone. This state is when our abilities are sharpened and we are capable of great feats seemingly without any effort. The fourth state is deep awakening, beyond

the Zone. This state is said to be rarely attained, the likes of Buddha and Jesus being among those who have achieved this superior state of consciousness known as the point behind the veil in Om.

Consciousness is the awareness of awareness. The level of awareness varies in accordance to the level of consciousness. Most are aware they are seeing, but are they aware of their thinking? Are you aware of the thought processes taking place within? The more we step back and observe our emotions and thoughts instead of simply being them the more aware we become.

Carl Jung said, "A healthy man does not torture others -generally it is the tortured who turn into torturers." What is customary is often just that and beyond tradition has no merit and to outsiders might be considered tortuous. Yet just being aware of awareness and asking yourself am I repeating what was done to me can change this, just being aware can change everything.

Our minds are like great cities of thinking and feeling. And like the island of Manhattan, the avenues and streets of thinking and feelings intersect the islands of our minds. When we are on the block the city looks one way, across the river it looks entirely different and from above, seeing the entirety, it is another thing entirely. Try to cross the river or fly a plane to become more aware of your entire self, not just your comfortable attitude or neighborhood.

36. Learn about the power of self. And expand your own power. Practice and refine the things you are good at and gravitate to. Try also to better your abilities at unfamiliar things. Do not let other tell you what you are good at or what you are capable of doing. People will tell you that you are too young or too old, that you are under qualified or overqualified, but only you can know your abilities. Yet most people do not know our true ability, partly because we have believed the limits imposed on us by others. Our perception limits us more than anything. Elevate it and elevate your capabilities. Learn about how much time and energy we can waste thinking about what others might do and learn not to waste your time and energy doing so. Instead conceive you. Allow yourself to be your own motivator and do not accept the distractions and degrading thoughts of others.

37. Never let yourself be tricked. See 34 – 36. Don't allow people to get into your head with their selfish suggestions. Whether it is in a basketball game or in life don't let people get into your head and convince you of something about yourself or them that will allow them to take advantage of you. Be discerning.

There are four types of lies directly related to the four operations of arithmetic. Mathematical approaches can assist in making sense of the unpredictable dynamics, making sense of and finding the truth. Outright conjuration and total denial of fact are the obvious two types of lies. But the advanced lies are more nuanced and subtle as opposed to outright addition and total subtraction of information.

The first type of lie is addition of information. Sometimes the addition of a small bit of information can change the story entirely. The second type of lie is the subtraction of information. The removal of small but key components can result in entirely different meaning. The third type of lie is multiplication of information. Exaggerations of situations connected with the story as well as exaggerations of extraneous information are included in the presentation to dilute it. The fourth type of lie is division of information. The facts are interlaced with disconnects and the significance of information is separated. Watch out for such euphemistic and dysphemistic presentations downplaying or exaggerating.

There are many ways to tell if someone is lying. Any changes in their normal approach could be signs of lies. Stuttering, touching the face, and speaking messily are signs of lies. See if they can or will look you in the eye during silence or speech. Perhaps the best way to detect lies is to extensively dissect the situation and choose not to be reactive so we don't slip into lies. A liar usually is defensive when confronted about lies as opposed to people with truth who tend to become offensive if falsely accused. Accused liars love to have the conversation changed whereas accused liars who are actually truth tellers tend to want to stay on the subject so as to prove their truth.

38. Pretend to be in the fourth state of consciousness. Pretend to be in the state of Buddhahood and Christ consciousness for a time. Experiment with being ultra-compassionate and considerate and graceful toward your fellow man and your surroundings. Silently wish positive happiness for people you encounter and actively

and openly assist those you come across, strangers and more importantly people whom you know, with whom there is tension.

We are all impermanent mortals subject to death. Realize for a moment that you could have died before. And then imagine returning and being here now, with all the opportunity to help others and positively influence your surroundings. The experiment of helping others like a saint or enlightened being can help bring about experience of how changing one's mindset can change everything.

Pretend to be what you are afraid of being or doing. If you are afraid of being the hero pretend to be the hero. If you are afraid to speak in front of the crowd pretend you are an eloquent speaker. If you are afraid to speak with someone you're attracted to pretend to be the most dashing and debonair individual she has ever met. Never act, but be, only first pretend to be and then you will see people react to you as if you were a confident hero or what have you. This is of course a delicate procedure which requires dipping your toes, then your feet, before wading in such waters. Pretend in order to evolve yourself not to deceive others. Imagination is king. Use it and be it.

39. Remember beauty is achieved in minimization and simplicity, as is long term strength. Do not use artificial additives to beautify oneself, like makeup, hair gels and dyes for these things tend to be toxic and will age you unnecessarily. In seeking to become strong there are many supplements and many are in the same way unnecessary and in the end are toxic. One can only digest so much protein and your body can only handle so much supplements. The less refined your diet is, the stronger you will become and the less accompaniments to your beauty, the more beautiful you will remain. The simplest way to retain beauty is to smile. All smiling happy people are met as beautiful. No matter how much of an hourglass figure you have and no matter how perfect of a pentagram your face forms the most powerful and simple form of beautification is smiling.

40. Be vigilantly aware of the difference between institutions and individuals, as well as the difference between materials and individual life. Machines cannot like you back and institutions cannot be your friend. Only living beings breathe and face mortality.

Legend has it that when the Hopi met someone in the dark they would ask, 'Who goes there?' If it were a fellow Hopi they would simply respond, 'I am me.' Be like the Hopi, the people of peace, be you, and consider others around you as brothers.

When you're asked who you are by someone in the dark, do not identify yourself as the uniform you wear or the building you work in or an institution of any sort. The Hopi also referred to people who lose their way and become selfish and hungry for something other than themselves, say people who identify themselves through an institution, as people of two hearts. Follow your own heart, not the supposed hearts of mechanized institutions.

The Hopi, meaning people of peace, from the Southwest United States, settled in the arid desolation of Arizona because of the fact that the land is so foreboding. It is arid and the topsoil blows around making agriculture extraordinarily difficult. They settled there because they knew that settling there meant they would always need each other. The Hopi theorized that when people do not need those around them, they don't think about others and become more self-absorbed and more selfish.

All Native American Indians famously never wasted anything. And when they killed an animal, not only did they use every part of it, but they respected the animal and its surroundings. They approached beings and their environment with reverence. Today corporate animal raising is astoundingly harmful to the animals, the area, and all who consume it.

The following are Hopi proverbs:

"All people without faith in themselves cannot survive."

"All dreams spin out from the same web."

"Eating little and speaking little can hurt no man."

"If we dig precious things from the land, we will invite disaster."

41. Stay clean. The simplest of soaps are the most effective, the healthiest and the least toxic. Soaps made with clay, salts and minerals are the best for one's skin. The

earth, the dirt is not filth. Filth is manmade and sometimes it even smells good. Speaking of smelling good, body odor is caused by bacteria on the skin consuming the sweat, not sweat itself. Use natural deodorants scents and crystal mineral salts. Avoid working with or working for corporations that manufacture toxic substances for our cleanliness and the cleanliness of others. Shower and bathe frequently but use small amounts of soap and especially shampoo. Shampoo your hair infrequently, your hair and scalp will be healthier.

Our skin is porous and permeable. The more natural the soaps and products you use the less detoxification your body has to work through after simple activities like taking a shower, swimming in the pool or washing the dishes. Your body automatically will expend energy in attempting to detoxify what many consider regular products, so the less toxic products you use the more energy you will have.

42. Accept that there is the unknown and unseen to surpass fear and ignorance. Proceeding using only the five senses as your guide and nothing more, will limit you. The best way to learn new things is to first accept there are new things to learn and the best way for anything resembling miraculous or magical to enter your life is if you accept that there are things at work beyond the five sense comprehension and outside of the scope of what is considered normal human faculties. We are trained to see physical action and reactions, however there are things at work that are most often untraceable, at least through our five senses and science. An example of unknowns in known interactions is that of biology. There are biological circumstances at play in the world that are undetectable and at the same time undeniable. There are also astrological and spiritual influences on us which are potentially equally powerful, but for the most part, intangible. Astronomically speaking the moon can move the oceans. So it's not such a stretch to contemplate that it and other celestial bodies may affect our emotional tides, our inner waters.

Children often are afraid of the dark, but they are really afraid of what they don't see. They are really afraid of the experience of the unknown. Adults know better than to be afraid of the darkness, but there are many points in time where other forms of unknowns can frighten adults like the dark does young children often just as unreasonably so. A walk in the dark often relives the fear of it. Buddha and many other meditators meditated in cemeteries so as to relieve fear, not of death but fear in total, for fear of the unknown or otherwise, results in being closed minded and closed off to energy, where as lacking fear leads to openness.

43. Use your mind power. Every culture throughout recorded time realized the power of the mind. The Hindu yogis who conceived the macrocosmic and microcosmic divinity of 108 and who calculated the speed of light did so through meditation. The American Indian shamans sought great medicine from their ancestors to find game or other advice. The aboriginal Australians traditionally walk and talk with spirit guides in what's called the dreamtime or dreaming. The idea of the dreaming is similar to the boundless space of timelessness or the Akashic field. In fact there is no aboriginal word for time. Think about having power to perceive the trinity of time displayed in 108 and the unsaid timelessness of its combination.

The U.S.A. government initiated the remote viewing program and perhaps something more accurately described as remote influencing program to counter the psychic development programs of the U.S.S.R. during the Cold War. Supposedly the first reading they did, of a giant mechanical crane, turned out to be highly accurate.

The first step to remote viewing is asking the specific question. Then listening and focusing. Draw or write what you see. Don't guess, ask. When listening one must learn to discern your own projections or conjurations, your wants or fears with true remotely viewed reflections. Learn to be open always so as to be more likely to be a vessel for remotely viewed reflections. The more reflections you perceive the easier it becomes to differentiate them from your own conjurations. The mind is a projector, whereas the heart is mirror. Close your ego thinking and open your heart.

44. Learn the difference between knowledge and wisdom. "To attain knowledge, add things every day. To attain wisdom, remove things every day." ~ Lao Tzu.

Even when the world was vastly simpler without the complications of environmental degradation, measure of one's knowledge was the complexity and depth of thought, while measure of wisdom was simplicity and breadth of action. Learning something as well as many things means very little if one can find remains incapable to contemplate the things or create new news things new applications or old applications which work better for self and surroundings.

A hollow mind might know many things, but few ways to apply what's known. A full mind might know only one thing, but many ways to apply what is known. In most long forms of tai chi there are 108 movements with innumerable variations and applications. Learning the entire form is gaining knowledge. Learning how to apply the movements is wisdom. What good would be learning the entire form without any understanding of application? Perhaps learning just one movement and numerous ways to apply it would be better. One must find balance between what one knows and the application of that knowledge.

45. Be confident. Stand straight and look people in their eyes. Put a light smile on your face and relax. Frequently the loudest people are overcompensating for lacking confidence. Lightly smile in a confident manner and people tend to smile back and offer you time to speak. It takes confidence to lightly smile in stressful and adverse situations, so much in fact that a smile can squash adversity. It throws people off, amazes others and makes adversaries question their being adversarial.

People gravitate to people reaching for the stars and it takes confidence to do so. People tend not to gravitate to people reaching out to them, they frequently think they are going to be grabbed. If you touch a moth or butterfly the oils on your hands soak its wings ruining it, you have to allow butterflies to touch you, to land on you. Be confident and lightly smile and the beauty of butterflies will come to you.

As long as you practice 44 you will have reason for being confident. Know that the more you devote yourself to any practice, be it snowboarding, tai chi or the Five Tibetan Rites of Rejuvenation, you will gain confidence in knowing your enhanced ability and perhaps more importantly from knowing the level of commitment it took to enhance that ability. Remember too it is a spiraling effect: the more you better yourself, the more confident you become and the more you better yourself.

Be confident in yourself and don't believe in Santa. I jest, what I mean to suggest is to look within, not to tradition. Do not look to the outside traditional world for inspiration or insight, for such is in you. Do not believe what you are presented and born into. Do not support the status quo and the mind state of all those who insist on maintaining their own status quo. Remember that the walls that surround you were once not there and will one day not be there. The doorways in life you seek to open often do not just open if you wait there long enough. And sometimes even going through the hoops to obtain the correct key or passcode won't get you through. Sometimes people will try to lock you out, and further build walls around you or between you and the door. Practically every door that opened for me in life was opened only after I managed to put my foot in the doorway. And all walls built up around me crumbled when I walked away from them. There is always a way through every door and every wall has a weak point too. When someone builds walls around you it is often best just to walk away. If you have to get through the walls built around you do not fight them, be confident. In confidence you can find stillness and when you find stillness you are able to responsibly respond rather than re-acting out reaction. Confident stillness alone can throw people off so much they will yield their aggression or interruption just because of that. Often such wall builders are looking for reactions and when there is none they crumble.

Sometimes when we attempt to accomplish reaching for the stars we fall or get hit. Everyone who tries gets hit. Many take that first hit and then quit like it's not worth it. Sometimes the trick is to get hit again and then it's like there is no other choice but to commit. The difference between success and failure is just confident commitment.

46. Avoid being upset over loss. Very few things can hurt as much as losing someone close to you, whether they pass away, move away or for whatever reason they're no longer around. The pain of losing a friend or loved one is comparable to nothing and rarely does one completely recover from such a loss, there is always scarring. But when you lose an object do not become upset. Nothing can overturn and collapse your balance easier than yourself. In Buddhism it is believed our desires and attachments lead to all suffering. Let go of your desires and attachments and you let go of suffering. Do not lend your emotions to material objects. Do not be upset over something replaceable or something that was never alive. People can be so materialistic that the loss of an item will upset them more than the object was ever worth, more than the loss could ever hurt.

The reason monks go on retreats to seek silence is to face their inner demons and also to seek silence so they are not distracted or upset by outer demons. Our capabilities can be so greatly and negatively altered by being upset that it is difficult to say where we would all be if we were not burdened with illogical feelings of loss or guilt of the lingering or occasional sort. Being upset reduces your capability. Conversely being too excited about something blurs clarity.

47. Share. The reason humanity has evolved is part biological and part societal. We are cooperators. As good of a damaging weapon the fist can be, the hand is primarily designed to hold things and then let them go. The hand holds so that we can give. The hand is the best design on the planet, for giving, not for fighting. If man were designed to fight rather than give, to destroy rather than build we would have more ferocious appendages. It is in our nature to cooperate and assist. Because too many people have sought to have too much that they cannot use, too many people go without. There are few things that are as rewarding as sharing. It is in our nature to share and cooperate. We must be trained to do otherwise. Those who are destructive and those who do not give have been trained to be that way and are not being themselves.

48. Realize strength is gained through adversity. The more difficulty you go through, the more trials you face the easier things become. The longer you run or swim the longer and better you will be able to do so. The more weight you lift the more weight you will be able to lift. The more you climb the better you will be able to do so and the higher you will be able to go.

We may gain strength through adversity directly and indirectly. Try taking a snow bath so as to build your ability to generate heat. Contract your muscles and utilize Taoist reverse breathing to absorb and keep heat. On inhalation contract and pull in your abdomen. On exhalation relax your belly to normal position. Just as the benefits of weight training or bone tapping come from taking the time to act in a manner that presently does nothing but cause some discomfort so as to gain future strength. Weight lifting benefits through pain as does bone tapping. Through weight training one is less susceptible to injury —over time. And with practicing bone patting one develops an iron shirt or armor so that one is stronger and less likely to be injured as well.

49. Understand awareness in order to enhance. We are capable of highly tuned (or rather in-tuned intuitive) awareness. The more open and accepting we are the more capable of awareness we are, the less guilt and fear, the more awareness. The first level of awareness is of self. The second level of awareness is of bodies outside self, birds, trees, and other people included. The third level of awareness is sensitivity to understanding how your body interacts with other bodies. Tai chi practice enhances sensitivity so that one is aware of the tiniest insect landing on you. These levels of awareness are all physical, related to self, others and the interaction of, or interoception, exteroception and proprioception. The fourth level of awareness is metaphysical precognition and intuition whereupon one is so sensitive to changes inside and outside that one can conceptualize things before they are apparent to most, before they even actualize, the fourth aspect is preproprioception. Tai chi, kung fu and similar meditative movements develop preproprioception sensitivity. One can be so sensitive that one can understand exactly what is happening before it happens in interaction with surroundings or elsewhere intuitively.

These four levels of awareness, for me, ring as counterparts or correlations to the Buddhist concepts of the Four Immeasurables. The Four Immeasurables are love of self, love for others, love for the happiness of others and love of all things in equanimity. The more open one is the closer one gets to loving all things in equanimity the more awareness one has access to. Without the Four Immeasurables openness and access to the higher levels of awareness is practically impossible -more on the Four Immeasurables later.

Everything is energy and vibration. In tai chi, part of practicing slowly is so one pays attention to every minute detail as well as the big picture of the movement. A more subtle reason for being gentle and slow is so we never limit ourselves in knowing how fast we can go, or how intense we can flow. The amount of energy vibrating inside and outside is enormous and yet our physical bodies can only go so fast, vibrate so much and detect so much. When we constantly physically train for speed and strength we 'learn' or place limits on our abilities and convince ourselves we cannot go past our limits we place. By moving slowly we enhance our awareness and never learn our highest rate of speed, and never place a limit on our ability.

We place limits on our intuitive awareness, our ability to access preprioception, in the same way. We allow ourselves to be limited by understanding and holding onto our limits, by reinforcing the idea we only have a limited number of senses and are capable of only sensing most tangible and gross forms. In fact, when we disavow our limitations we can access more speed, strength and awareness of energy and vibration.

50. Grow a garden. Grow a plant by a window. There is nothing more rewarding as turning nothing into something and hardly anything is done so directly, as growing fresh food. There are few activities beyond growing food which bring you more in tune with your environment. If you cannot grow a garden see if you can Johnny Appleseed plants anywhere where there is not a plant, whether annual or perennial. Grow something, somewhere.

Obtain house plants to get in touch with growing and to clean the air indoors. The Spider plant, Boston fern, areca palm, money plant, mother in law's tongue, English ivy, aloe vera, snake plant, marginata, peace lily and Chinese evergreen all improve the air quality indoors. Try an indoor edible herb garden.

Practice the meditation of hugging a tree. Stand with your feet about shoulder width apart and your arms in front of you with your palms open as if you were holding large ball of energy mutually shared by you and the tree and that this energy is feeding the tree that feed the world with oxygen and at the same grounding you energy. Literally hug a tree with your forehead touching it and your hands pressing the tree.

Meditate on being a tree. Stand completely still and rooting yourself into the earth or floor. Stand with knees slightly bent, should width apart and try holding your hands at your sides or in front of you facing your dantien/naval, or outstretched to your sides with palms facing in or out, in front of you or above your head with palms out. Be balanced and hold still in meditation, as if a tree.

Sit under a tree, facing it or not, and try to feel connection with the tree. Imagine that the tree and you are intermingling energy and that the tree being tapped and rooted more directly to the earth and being more capable of photosynthesis is more rooted to the earth and more in touch with the sun and therefore can offer more energy which you can use. Meditate on feeling oneness with the tree and feeling it. Remember that Buddha gained enlightenment under a tree.

In contrast to spending time with plants, spend time with animals. Perhaps reading facial movements can be bettered simply by spending time with animals and observing them and with them. Look into their eyes and alternatively look at them with your eyes unfocused and take in their whole being. The expression of animals and humans are similar only humans can lie with their words. But sometimes you can see through what people say by what people do. And sometimes what you see or what you think you see physically is a psychic hint that you noted and interpreted with your eyes as a facial tick or this or that.

A great teacher once told me, 'many people in the world choose to work, I choose to meditate. In this world you can work or you can meditate.' If you have time to work, go to work, prepare for work and talk about work, then you definitely have time to grow plants and/or meditate sometimes.

51. Break patterns. Do different things and do what you do regularly, differently. Simply walking on different paths or approaching the same systems in alternate manners to the traditional approach seeds new thoughts and sprouts dendrites. Experiencing things differently and of course doing different things sprouts dendrites, an important part of nerve cells. Dendrites transmit information throughout the cell and then signals are transmitted to dendrites of neighboring cells. In a millisecond information is understood from external signals, sights, sounds, touch and chemical input, through dendrites. Dendrites look like trees and the word comes from the Greek word for tree. The more developed they are, the more developed they become, the more they branch out, like trees. If you're not training, you're being trained. And normally in the process of not training you're be trained to be dulled.

52. If it is at all possible to conduct your daily business in alignment with solar time rather than the time on the clock, do it. Try it if only for brief episodes. Try to think of yourself timelessly. Get rid of your alarm clock, wrist watch and cell-phone. Turn your clocks to face the wall or change the time on them to make yourself unaware of it. Do not pay attention to the clock, but understand the calendar and the natural cycle if and when you can. This can put you in touch with the cyclical nature of time instead of the linear distraction of its presentation. Consciousness is comparably cyclical. Being in

touch with time without tools brings you closer to be in touch with consciousness. Forgetting about time conversely allows us to be present which builds awareness of consciousness.

Try to remove all numerical connections for a time. People who choose not to meditate, to sit comfortably -but not too comfortably in meditation, actually meditate more than people who choose to contently meditate. Mostly people meditate on numerical ideas; money, time and bodyweight among them. Further most people who do not choose to sit comfortably –but not too comfortably in meditation do in fact meditate, only in a way which invariably inhibits instead of expanding consciousness. People will sit contemplating time and money for days at a time and will sit –too comfortably and watch television for hours at a time. These activities are akin to meditation only with inverse results, instead of becoming aware of ourselves we are taken outside ourselves.

In order to wake up early without an alarm clock simply drink a significant amount of water before bed. Two or three glasses of water before bed will allow you to wake up early easily.

53. Eat local, organic and free trade if possible. Support family farms or start one. Certified organic makes the system of agriculture, for all extents and purposes fair trade. Workers are fairly not required to use toxins which jeopardize their health and the health of the consumers. Eating organic reduces the toxins in the environment as well as in yourself. The toxic runoff of fertilizer and fecal matter from conventional, i.e. large scale corporate agriculture is ruining rivers and whole oceans.

If you have a chronic problem or dis-ease in any form of severity from acne to arthritic pain, or even Alzheimer's disease try to change the diet to chiefly organic, wild, or sustainable agriculture. Perhaps the problem is exposure to toxins or perhaps the problem is exacerbated by the exposure to toxins, often present in foods. Try an organic vegan diet and see the difference.

Eat sparingly and diversely. The greater the assortment of fruits, vegetables, legumes and grains one eats the better access to more nutrients one gains. Do all that you can to be vegan. Vegans can eat practically all they want without becoming overweight, just no animal products.

Occasional consumption of meat and dairy might be ok, depending on where it is from and what it ate during its life. However consumption of less animal products exposes you to less bioaccumulative toxins. Eating less meat will allow your body to heal quicker and be stronger for longer. Meat production in the U.S.A. results in environmental horrors as well. Raising small numbers of animals is good for the environment, but raising thousands is monumentally devastating to the surrounding region.

54. Seek balance. Balancing ourselves is essential to being in The Zone. Building balance is like building a table, even if there is a smooth surface, if one of the legs is out of balance the function of the table is limited. Balancing self is like putting four legs together to make a table. In carpentry the legs just have to be the same size, in life the four legs or four aspects that must be balanced are the physical, mental, spiritual and natural. Be humble and noble. Be kind and strong. Be generous and protective. Be in the present, not the past or the future.

Cherish old friends and seek new friends. You cannot make old friends. And at the same time your new friends are more likely to reflect your current mind state.

Yoga, tai chi, chi gung, walking and even weight lifting all end up being good for you because they first bring balance to the system. After one is balanced enhanced energy, true wellbeing and strength can be realized and utilized. All physical systems first regulate and balance so that you can be your true, capable self. This is true for studies, relationships and in dealing with most anything in our surroundings. Apply balanced thinking to meditative movement and living.

55. Practice transmutation of sexual energy into life energy. This is a little spoken of often hidden secret of tai chi, chi gung, yoga and the Five Tibetans. More recently Wilhelm Reich whose work on what he called orgone (from orgasm) energy suffered the greatest book burning in U.S.A. history.

Developing sexual energy and turning it into life energy is so taboo still that it is the least often taught aspect of energy development and possibly the most important. Despite mention in practically all practices it often goes unmentioned perhaps because of puritanical dogma and leniencies. The trick for men to build sexual energy, increase testosterone and enhance one's overall vitality is to withhold orgasm. One can have sex to the point of climax, but not actually release the orgasm. When men build up their sexual energy in such a way they can build up the women's.

There are ways for women to transmute their sexual energy on their own only I am unaware of specifics beyond the following. The art of building sexual energy in this way takes practice, like anything. One can develop on this, having sex to the point of orgasm without ejaculating, pleasing yourself or your partner and initiating transmutation of sexual energy into life energy. One can perform this process through, let's say, self-actualization or preferably with a partner.

Celibacy is suggested by many traditions as the way to build sexual energy. Others point to building the energy through practicing meditative sex to the point of climax only without actually ejaculating. To build sexual energy into life energy practice meditative sex to the point of climax and then withhold, and imagine the energy transmutation. It takes a certain concentrated relaxation to do however it brings about feelings of ecstasy without ejaculation. This practice transmutes energy and also develops self-control, in every aspect. In yoga, practicing celibacy is part of the retention of bodily fluids. In tai chi and chi gung the process is referred to as the transmutation of fluids, reversing the flows of the waters, dialects of the same language.

Once you have withheld remained celibate and/or withheld ejaculation for at least a couple of days, the longer the better and once you have practiced the Five Rites of Rejuvenation enough, to where you can remember the order in which they are performed and can perform 21 repetitions with relative ease you can assist transmutation of sexual energy into life energy by including the Sixth Rite of Rejuvenation. It is the only Rite that should be done no more than 4 or 5 times, 3 being plenty. Celibacy or withholding ejaculation is not a requirement, but enhances the benefits of the Sixth Rite. Practicing the Five Rites for at least two weeks is recommended or just doing them with ease.

The sixth Tibetan is extremely powerful and should be treated as such. Inhale in the same position as the bandha in between each Rite, hands at your hips. On the exhalation reach for your knees, maintaining slight bend in the knees and arch in the back and exhale completely through the mouth. Evacuate all oxygen to the point the diaphragm is contracted. Rise back up, maintaining contraction, to the starting position used in between each Rite without inhaling. Do not inhale on the way up. Hold your breath as long as you can in this position, just before you make yourself angry. And inhale. Take a breath in between the next Sixth Rite and then repeat.

Chi gung and tai chi can also transmute the sexual energy, the Five and Six Tibetan Rites are just more directly vigorous. One form of chi gung which raises sexual energy is to cup your right hand in your left hand at you dantien (left in right palm for females) and on inhalation raise them in front of you as if caressing a ball of energy at your belly so they now face downward. Return them down on exhalation so that the hands are cupped facing up. Repeat this for a few minutes slowly and meditatively.

Now enhance this same idea only on inhalation bring the hands up as if splashing the face and keep going reaching to the sky with your hands transforming to prayer position at your face and then let your arms blossom up and then reaching outward like a blossoming flower. Now reverse this movement on the exhalation. With your hands outstretched return them to above your head in prayer and then as if diving into water, your head follows your hands down to the floor and if flexible pointing through and slightly behind the legs. Now very slowly inhale, hands go from prayer to cupped as if bringing up energy, until reaching the face and then repeat the cycle a few times.

Exploring sexuality with love is a beautiful thing and releases you from the otherwise constraining feeling of loneliness. But basing your identity solely on your sexuality or existing solely to express your sexuality is not healthy. Orgasms can enhance your wellbeing as can celibacy, and Taoist or yogi retention of bodily fluid techniques as well. The purpose of doing either is to raise one's energy and awareness up from desire at the root chakra to your third eye and crown chakras, to transmute earthly sexual energy coiling upwards into higher life force energy, kundalini, chi or prana.

56. Be happy. Sometimes for various reasons this is, as the cliché goes, easier said than done. If all sadness is a combination of simple chemical processes than it is important to note that the B vitamins, from proper sources, can cure depression as well as other sicknesses. And simple malnourishment and dehydration can hinder positivity which can be alleviated with quality food and water.

If all depression is a spiritual matter meditation on happiness and thinking positively can assist in ascension of one's perspective. Meditating on happiness can lead to happiness all by itself. Be accommodating to others and say yes to others more often. Do not ignore the potential biological impacts, in this case lacking nutrition, or emotional impacts, of say lacking love, resulting in your state of being.

Being humorous, funny and invoking laughter is considered to be the highest state of being. Just as smiling is infectious and can change situations for the better laughter can do the same. Laughter not only causes physical vibrations and heightened openness to energy it is infectious goodness. Try laughing yoga. Practice doing whatever positions you are comfortable with breathing in slowly and then laughing out loud during exhalations. Laughing yoga reveals the infectious nature of laughter. At first a group doing laughing yoga laughs willfully, then uncontrollably. Laughter is like light in this way. Laughter and light both take over everywhere they start a spark.

Laughing makes people laugh. No one is as well-loved, as easily accepted into new groups or as quickly forgiven as a humble and knowledgeable good humored individual. Nothing is as good for you and those around you as well intentioned humor.

At the very core of our being we are absolutely in control of how we feel at all times. We are in control of how we think and more importantly how we feel. Whenever you say to yourself or say aloud that 'he/she makes me feel this/that way,' you are saying that this or that person is in control of how you feel. You are submitting to the idea that others are in control. To take control of your emotions and chaotic thinking always build your power to do so. You make yourself feel the way you do through your perspective, always, no exception.

"Mind precedes all mental states. Mind is their chief; they are all mind-wrought. If with a pure mind a person speaks or acts happiness follows him like his never-departing shadow." ~Buddha

57. Learn the power of yes and alternatively the power of no. Self-actualization and self-determination are frequently instigated by using the power of one reliant or defiant word, yes or no. The power of one person saying something as simple as 'yes' or 'no' can never be underestimated. Our speech is our power and one word can change what thousands of people or what everyone thinks, says and does. Try to encourage creativity and positivity with yes. And alternatively make sure to counter destruction and negativity with no.

58. Cooperation is more productive than competition. Only during games is competition beneficial as a form of training for real world cooperation or action. Cooperation is beneficial in the real world. This is true in most any kind of relationship and is observable in most every aspect of nature.

People and our institutional collectives are the only animals and systems that destroy resources without the need to do so, the only being that acquires, steals and kills without the need to do so, solely to possess the actual thing or experience of destroying it.

59. Learn emergency action. Be prepared. If you are lost in unknown territory, fashion a walking stick/staff to help move and help fend off any randomly aggressive creature, but just give them room and you should be fine. Look for a river and follow it downriver. Unless you know otherwise this will likely lead you to assistance.

Hydrogen peroxide induces vomiting if you or someone or pet are poisoned. As an extreme last resort in order to possibly stop an infection, eat undisturbed dirt which might contain antibiotics. Colloidal silver can kill various topical and internal infections as well as boost one's overall immunity.

If you are injured do not just lie around. Move what you can. When the aged and infirmed begin practicing chi gung for healing an injury or easing living, the first thing they need to do and sometimes the only thing they need to do is practice ringing the bell, the primal tai chi warm up of gently swiveling. The other movement that accompanies or sometimes is a preliminary is simple, gentle hip rotations without exertion. These two movements can initiate healing and general ease, if they can be done without pain of course.

Stay hydrated. Boil water for ten minutes to assure you kill all the little nasty creatures which could upset you. Use a bag of sand to filter water. A sock with sand makes an excellent water filter. Drink your own urine if you are in a position where you might dehydrate and die. If you constantly drink chlorinated water let some of your drinking water sit overnight, this way the chlorine has a chance to evaporate. Constant exposure to any chemical is likely negative, chlorine especially so.

60. Challenge your assumptions and do not judge harshly and absolutley. By challenging your perspective yourself, you can expand your horizons and ultimately refine your perspective. Doing so leads to the understanding that we are all improvable. As adults we do not share the same understandings as we did as young children or teenagers. Our assumptions were challenged and thereafter refined. This process should never stop.

Prejudiced thinking, prejudging, is about the most foolish way of being, especially when the prejudgment is based on something like appearance. One would never judge the inside of a house based on the door to the house being a familiar door.

I paraphrase an old allegory I heard once that demonstrates how frequently we assume and prejudge and how foolish it is to do so: There was a man walking along the beach. As he was walking on the beautiful and serene coastline he happened upon thousands of sandflies. The sandflies were abuzz, hopping and flying about in a scattered condition. The man kept on walking enjoying the beauty of the view and as went he couldn't help but think of the sandflies. They were on the shoreline of the beautiful ocean, at the transition point of land and sea and now the sun was setting. They probably only live a day or so and the sun was setting. And they probably never can appreciate the beauty they were immersed in. He started back and came across the sandflies' camp. They were jumping and flying about. He stopped to watch them. After he stopped for a moment, so did they. Their erratic hopping turned into a calm interaction. He realized he had stirred them. There are three initial lessons to keep in mind from this. You affect things around you without even trying. Two, sometimes appearances lead to the wrong conclusions. And three, we all can be like the sandflies and the man on the shoreline of vivid beauty.

People often are so caught up in their experiences and their view of the beach that you can ask them a question or mention a thing and because their thoughts dwell in preconceptions they will answer as if in another moment concerning another subject. Be in the moment so you can see what is really going on and understand individuals as they really are without the hindrance of prejudgment. Children are the best observers because they do not prejudge, but simply openly observe. Look at things as a child.

Realize many people will judge you sternly to the point of outright hypocrisy. And frequently people will judge you like New England Puritans are said to have judged accused witches. They would throw witches into turbulent waters and if they drowned they were not a witch if they survived they were guilty of being a witch and then sentenced. People will figuratively throw you into the waters or build a wall around you as a test to see your reaction. And in the case of the accused witches whether they pass or fail people pass harsh judgment.

61. Never work too hard and always work toward your dream, don't just tag along onboard someone else's dream. There is so much more to life than working and there is so much more work to do beyond working for monetary measured success in someone else's game plan. If you are able to concentrate your efforts on things which build toward something instead of working on someone else's building for the sole end of money, do so. Follow your youthful dreams for a time. And remember this Chinese saying I paraphrase, "It's never too late, until you no longer have saliva in your mouth." This means as long as you are breathing you can do something, as long as there is fluid in your mouth you have power and potential.

62. Be open to connection with that outside yourself. Understand that everything is made up of the same materials and all these materials are all the same age, around 14 billion years old. Understand that the forces of gravity and electromagnetic current make up an ethereal sea across space and time and that consciousness too permeates similarly through all space and time and that you are a part of the sea of consciousness, that you are affected by it and affecting it.

Finding connection with others results in the best feelings and finding connection with others helps us connect with the sea of timelessness. Realization of a connection in a scientific manner, through the shared air and shared chemical and mineral components, can help us realize our connection on a spiritual manner with each other, god, earth and the Akashic field.

In order to find connection one needs to imagine the connection. Scientific information only assists in this. And then one has to engage connection with compassion. In order to be open to connection with yourself connect with others and in order to connect with others connect with yourself. Connect by practicing forgiveness and compassion toward yourself and others. Be open to total, equal compassion with love for everything in equanimity. When are open to complete compassion, which means compassion for who/what once angered you, you are open to intuition. You can gauge how open one is to connection by how compassionate one thinks and acts.

Forgiveness allows us to be open to energy including intuitive energy. If one seeks elevated understanding, one's questions to be answered, one's mantras and prayers to reach fulfillment, one has to practice elevated thinking. The most ascended and elevated thinking is of forgiveness. It is very difficult to forgive all those who have done wrong. However, consider this comparison to allow for opening up to intuitive energy/more forgiveness. We are all subject to our biological impulses and societal steering. Some of us are more developed and we can now notice our biology and our mentality. We were all confused once and bettered ourselves and we are in the process of development at different stages. Holding anger and not forgiving people is often like being angry at dog for peeing on a post. No one in their right mind would be angry at a dog for doing such. This thinking can be applied to most any situation, not just dogs, but people, for often people who do things that anger us are simply acting out biological impulses or are steered and just confused as we all are to some measure. They are confused because they are closed and they are closed because they are angry so let them be an example to not be angry instead of cause anger.

108 can be utilized to help us remember the power of forgiveness; allow the one thing, the issue at present, to turn into nothing, into a nonissue, so as to open up to the infinite and not be stuck on one thing which does nothing.

63. Take care of yourself using natural preventatives and remedies. Hemp/marijuana oil helps healing of wounds and elimination of scarring. Aloe vera and honey are antiseptics for wounds and both work wonders topically and internally. Arnica Montana assists in recovery from twisting or bruising trauma or any injury where skin is not opened. Application of heat after a bruise of sprain keeps the blood flowing. After initial heat, repetition of equal application of heat and cold repetitively can do wonders. Sessions of ten to twenty minutes of heat followed by equivalent period of cold, repeated as many times as you can, ending with heat, does wonders. Cold showers or bathing in cold water can be healing. It increases blood flow, is cleansing, can boost testosterone in men and even alleviate depression.

Colloidal silver, grapefruit seed extract and garlic can be used to cure colds and alleviate minor infections. Colloidal silver carries and grapefruit seed extract might carry risks as does taking anything. Both should never be used for prolonged time periods and one should conduct research before taking anything, if possible. Even herbal supplements can be harmful when taken at the wrong time by the wrong people. So of course pharmaceuticals can be extremely dangerous with serious consequences.

I had a problem with swimmer's ear turning into ear infections. With experience I was able to counter the progression to infection ingesting grapefruit seed extract, inhaling eucalyptus oil and sublingual homeopathic remedies. I could feel the irritation progress into inflammation and then into infection. But I could counter such progression with grapefruit seed extract. If you feel irritation do something about it so it does not progress into something worse, take preemptive action. In the same way irritation leads to inflammation and then infection, bruising or impactful injury can lead to strain, sprain and worse. Take care that little things do not become worse.

The most powerful healer with the fewest number of side effects is your perspective. The idea that placebos have to be instituted into therapeutic research acknowledges the fact that sometimes perspective alone can initiate healing, especially when instigated to change perception through suggestion. The will of consciousness is perhaps the most powerful force, healing power included, in the universe. The most powerful medicines are preventatives. Eat natural herbs for flavor and health.

64. Apply the preactionary principle. The precautionary principle is the idea which arose after decades of worldwide environmental catastrophes. After numerous detrimental industrial blunders resulting in poisoned air, water and land, people, labeled environmentalists, came up with the idea of the precautionary principle. Consideration of past lies and mistakes led to the idea we ought to have precaution to maintain the environment instead of allowing experimental procedure. Essentially the precautionary principle asks four questions of industrial procedure: Is this necessary? Is there an alternative which is safer? What about the waste? What about if things go wrong?

The preactionary principle takes the precautionary principle to another level. The precautionary principle halts action whereas the preactionary principle takes action, frequently after something has been done which left the precautionary principle unconsidered. One can apply the preactionary principle on a personal or environmental level.

The preactionary principle is applicable on a personal level in the sense that if one sees a problem one is not responsible for one is still capable of doing something about it. Do something or at the very least say something about it. Do not let things go unsaid. Intuitively speaking if something about a person, place, or event disturbs you, avoid them or it. Environmentally speaking we should all take more action and speak up more on behalf of our planet, about the environmental problems consuming our planet. One could move a dangerous object before someone hurts themselves and move away from being around negative or dangerous people. Environmentally one can stop industrial procedures which may be implemented near you by speaking up at town meetings and/or boycotting institutions which do endanger the environment as much as possible.

The preactionary principle is meant to be performed out of care and responsibility. Most people react brutally and violently when action is taken. The preactionary principle is based on peace. The Bush Doctrine, which arguably set the tone for the beginning of the 21st century, is one of violence and extremism. The doctrine essentially states, if you are thinking about attacking us, we'll attack first.

The preactionary principle is not about striking first, but being the initiator of provoking peaceful positive action first. Taking peaceful positive proactive preaction helps cancel potentially negative situations for you and those around you. When the preactionary principle is upon you, you'll know. Normally it is during the moment when the voice in your head tells you that you don't have to do anything or say anything and a recollection of the feeling of when you were left to fend for yourself further tries to convince you to stay shut and move along. It is during these moments the following the preactionary principle can make heroes. Normally few questions are needed for the preactionary principle. In order to when to apply it simply wait for that voice, the ego or fear or whatever, to try to convince you to stay shut and move along. Four relevant questions to ask though are: Is this beneficial? Is this safe? Is there waste? Is this wrongful?

65. Consider the Seven Generations rule. Know the difference between wants and needs. The drive to acquire materials and through them status, has shaped the world into a place where greed is so commonplace it often goes unnoticed. People routinely seek to acquire wealth beyond what they could possibly ever utilize. In contrast to people wanting more than they need people also rarely help those truly in need. Help yourself always and help others if you can.

Realization of the difference between wants and needs and minimization of wants can alleviate suffering; the very base theory in Buddhism. Further realization of the wants and needs of others instead of leaving others unconsidered can alleviate the environmental burdens we leave behind.

The American Indian idea of the seven generations law considers the wants and needs of others in future generations by essentially asking, 'how will my actions impact the wants and needs of people seven generations from now?' This should be a primary question of collective operation, but it is not at all. There are also many corresponding predictions related to the seventh generation law which all state essentially that seven generations after the white man takes over Turtle Island (the name given to ~North America) dreadful environmental disasters would occur, birds would fall from the sky, the air would burn the eyes of men and the fish would die in the rivers they swam in and that the waters would turn red. The collective choices of the last seven generations have indeed resulted in such occurrences. And what will result from seven more generations of the status quo?

Today we have the commonly celebrated and wholly accepted idea of a life for completing bucket lists. Live for something other than a selfish bucket list, fulfillment of desires to be done before death. Follow a dream to do something bigger than oneself. Follow the dream of our ancestors to better the human predicament and help us alleviate the environmental damage that's been done in supposedly pursuing that end. This will take you to a mountain of adventure greater than the highest bungee jump.

"Live as if you were to die tomorrow. Learn as if you were to live forever." ~Gandhi

66. Please, thank you, forgive me and I love you are the most powerful sentiments and statements there are capable of squashing all sorts of confrontation. The four concepts of friendship can mend and bend. Stating and truly meaning these words can mend stressed and broken relationships and bend individuals toward positivity.

The traditional Polynesian concept of ho'oponopono communicates these concepts. The idea was practiced by healers and is said to communicate something to the effect of, 'I'm sorry, please forgive me, thank you, I love you.' As a meditation the saying is great stress reliever and as a practice can help solve problems. I'm sorry, please, thank you and I love you are powerful independently and together can inspire healing inwardly and outwardly. And remember; respect gets respect.

Today we need to be grateful and practice the art of forgiveness perhaps like no other time before because we have not been grateful or forgiving for so long. We need to be pleased with what we have and be thankful for what we obtain while initiating forgiveness and opening up an environment of love. The world needs a shift in human consciousness beginning with the four parts of Ho'oponopono, perhaps especially and most often forgiveness.

Forgiveness elevates, whereas an unforgiving mind state hinders degrades and at best keeps one stagnate. No matter the reasoning, letting go and forgiving allows you to open up instead of being closed. Forgiveness is release and allows for forward movement. When you are mature you don't become mad with a child for being messy, you show them how to eat without soiling their shirt. The same is applicable as we age and experience more complex situations with more subtle messes. The ability to forgive is a sign of maturity and the ability to be well and promote wellness.

Many national interests have been wrapped up in acquiring supreme weaponry including nuclear experimentation devices which inevitably are destroying the environment and could destroy totality near instantly. The procedure of nuclear experimentation is part of global the state of war, the world needs us to change our mind state to a state of peace and acceptance. All life on the planet requires we shift our mentality to one of loving kindness, so we are one with nothing between us, infinitely.

67. Maintain your body's alkalinity. Human blood should be slightly alkaline (7.35 - 7.45). Below or above this range means sickness. The body will compensate for acidic pH by using alkaline minerals. If your diet does not contain enough minerals to compensate, calcium and magnesium will be drawn from your bones to buffer the acidity. Foods resulting in alkaline environment are melons, all citrus, figs, raisins, greens, seeds, sea salt, coconut oil, apple cider vinegar, flax and hemp.

Consume probiotics. There are many probiotics one can consume which are not dairy based. Our biological functions are dependent and intertwined with the biological function of intestinal bacteria. Maintaining healthy flora is key to health and longevity. Kombucha, kim chi, sauerkraut, dark chocolate, miso soup, blue-green algae, spirulina, chlorella, coconut kefir and pickles are some foods beneficial to healthy intestinal environment. Think of the little things which make such a great contribution to existence, the tiny bacteria integrated within and the minute window of acidic and alkaline conditions we require for balance.

68. Release trapped energy. It's difficult to talk about the natural function of flatulence without laughing. And in all honestly both laughing and flatulency result in great relief and release. In fact if you have a stomach ache farting may be exactly what you need. Eastern medicine and established internal arts hold that trapped energy or elements cause unease or dis-ease including trapped air. I call the practice of releasing trapped air the secret Taoist farting technique, so as to laugh, but surely there is a much more beautiful phrase for it in one or another dialect. Stretch in the yoga position known as downward dog, facing the floor on one's knees and forearms or hands. Fart.

Rub your belly with your palm in circles thirty times or more, equally clockwise and counterclockwise when you wake up and when you go to the bathroom to prevent and alleviate indigestion or poor digestion. Sit up straight when you have a bowel movement, press on your feet or even squat. Our bodies our designed in a way we relieve ourselves more effectively squatting.

Remember to take time to breathe. Exhale deeply and imagine acids and gasses being evacuated.

Indigestion is often symptomatic of poor diet. And such slight dis-ease can be indicators that something is out of balance with emotional or biological causes and remedies. Sometimes though the dis-ease of indigestion and other similar mortal discomforts are caused by less traceable and tangible elements we call stress. The root of flowering stress is not the day to day events which throw us off balance, such stressors are just water to feed the plant. The roots of stress are emotional/thoughtful energy blockages we leave buried and ignored that are like triggers or buttons. Usually the blockages are from traumatic childhood events which take root because we could not understand or adequately contemplate the events. Sometimes we hold onto things too much. Just as sometimes we have too much energy.

On a less laughable note, often we undertake activity or consume products to increase our energy. The trick to gaining quality positive energy is eliminating negative unhelpful energy. The quality energy will flow when the blockages are relieved. Tai chi postures and the breathing concentrates more on release of energy through the hands so that quality energy can be generated from as little as being rooted. Eliminate the negative in order to assimilate the positive.

If you feel you have too much energy think about opening your palms and keeping them open throughout the day. Take a moment to meditate with your palms facing up, resting on your legs in a cross legged or seated position, or lying flat on your back. Imagine energy evacuating from out your hands. Use the cooling breathing technique where one enhances and prolongs the pause of the breath where one's lungs are empty.

69. Do not build unnecessarily. The problem with the white western world is building unnecessary contraptions to replace what was a system in perfectly fine, natural

working order. Many of our most obnoxious and dangerous inventions of the status quo are ruinous in this manner. Genetically modified organisms made to support franchise operations and replace natural seed hybridization is one such operation, nuclear power plants are another.

Never reduce yourself to expending energy in planning and enacting out plans to hurt or restrain others. This is psychopathic behavior. Cease thinking about others and comparing yourself to others and trying to defeat others. The time spent concerned with others could be spent improving yourself and your surroundings.

Hemp and marijuana were made illegal and whole industries, nearly entirely harmful to individuals and environment, sprouted up to replace the industrial and medicinal power plants. Hemp is the oiliest plant there is. Everything that can be produced from petroleum can be grown with hemp; including energy. Often the reason for building machinery is presented as a way to better individuals and the collective however mostly machinery is built to make money. Alternative energy systems are only alternative to the oligarchical structure of building unnecessarily to make money. On the global scale we need to grow more fuel like hemp and harvest more energy already present in the wind, waves, waters and Sun. Eat hemp. It is one of the few foods that provides everything humans need to live.

Remember that being athletic and artistic is creating something from nothing. While war, as well as the current energy systemization of petrol and nuclear, all make something into nothing.

70. Consume quality oils. Again avoid anything genetically modified as most canola, corn and soy oils are. One of the most difficult nutrients to obtain in the natural world is fat and oil. Coconut, olive, hemp, flax, avocado and sesame are some sources of higher quality oils than can replace cow milk butter and genetically modified corn, canola and soy oils. We are consciousness machines and our sinews operate with oil as a lubricant just like a typical automobile engine. The fats in oils are needed. Fat is not necessarily bad itself, too much of the wrong fats from the wrong oil however does have negative results. Ask people why they are more conscious of the oil they put in their car and less concerned with the oil they put into themselves.

71. Think about detoxification. We are constantly exposed to toxins like no other generation before us, by orders of magnitude in the thousands whether it is electromagnetic, radioactive or another vast array of toxins from petrolithic fueled culture. Consume detoxifying foods regularly. To effectively detoxify exercise and sweat, spend time in a sauna, eat sarsaparilla root, burdock root, niacin and fermented foods, bentonite clay, zeolite, charcoal, not necessarily at once of course. Drink plenty of clean water and a principally vegetarian diet. Drink physillium husk –mix with water and drink quickly before it coagulates.

72. Practice the process of acceptance, integration and transmutation in your thinking for healing and wellness. Think of the number 108. If you would like the feeling of oneness, of connection with self or others, one has to accept totality into oneness. If you reject anything you are limiting yourself and hurting yourself as one does in avoidance of reality whether not looking where you are going or not processing what led you to where you are. One must accept perceived negativity and integrate it in order to get passed it and surpass it. Integration mixes the positive and negative so that there is nothing to be counted or divided other than the oneness, so there is nothing blocking the movement of energy. Transmutation is turning limiting weakness into infinite strength. This can only be accomplished through acceptance and integration. This is the highest process of meditative movement and arguably in life.

This breakdown of 108, acceptance of all into one, of integration so nothing is blocking anything and transmutation of weakness into infinite strength, is the basic formula for healing love. When two people accept each other they become like one. When two become one nothing can stand between them. When there is nothing in between people love can create and heal infinitely. Love is acceptance, integration and transmutation. Healers the world over, who healed with their spiritual touch, all do so by seeing the perfection of the spiritual nature of all they encounter and in doing so are then able to heal through acceptance, integration and transmutation.

It is scientifically understood most of us only use a very small percentage of our mental capacity. Similarly, most people only open up their spiritual capacity in the about the same proportions or even less so. Most of us only use approximately 5% of our mental capacity and most of us are only open spiritually in the same tiny proportions. It's like we are asleep in a dark room on a bright sunny day with one window sealed by a very dark shade that only lets in a tiny sliver of light. Acceptance, integration and transmutation leads to opening up and letting in light and healing.

There are many practices that heal via the spiritual touch, like Jesus is said to have done. Joh Rei is one such healing practice with origins in Japan. There are also many individuals of all sorts of diverse practices and traditions who have been known to heal psychically or spiritually, despite the many kooks and quacks who also tout as much in fakery. It is a matter of being metaphysically, energetically and spiritually open, I believe.

72, three fourths of 108, is the number for God from Old Testament traditions and in the story of Jacob's Ladder he sees 72 steps on the ladder between Earth and Heaven. God in any form is the ultimate acceptor, integrator and transmutator. Interestingly The Bible speaks of 144,000 chosen people, 12,000 from 12 tribes. 144, which simplifies down to 9, is 72 multiplied by 2. Interestingly, 144,000 divided by 108 equals 1333.333333333333.

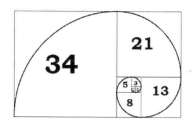

144 (108 is 36x3, 144 is 108+36) makes another significant appearance as the first three digit number illustrated in the Golden Mean or Fibonacci Sequence when beginning with 0. The Golden Mean is reflective of universal and individual mutuality, the idea that as above so below, that the micro reflects the macro. This correlates with the idea behind 108, like our inner orbit of breath and the outer orbit of the Earth around the Sun and Moon around the Earth.

The measurement associated with the Golden Mean is 1 and .618. The sequence used to demonstrate it is based on simple addition and proceeds like so: 0+1=1, 1+1=2, 2+1=3, 3+2=5, 5+3=8, 8+5=13, 13+8=21, 21+13=34, 34+21=55, 55+34=89, 89+55=144, 144+89=233, and on and on into infinity conceivably. If we continue with this pattern and then break down each number into its essence, 144 becoming 9 and 233 becoming 8 for instance, we see a pattern, where 0 is soon replaced with 9 in each subsequent first 25 digit set, and a 24 digit sequence presents itself infinitely, where each 24 digit sequence adds up to 108.

73. Face your fears. Nothing will build your character more than facing your fears. Nothing will build self-awareness more than finding out exactly what height you are afraid of and then proceeding to climb there and beyond. Many people do not know what they are afraid of because they don't go out of the mundane routine. Many people do not even realize what they are afraid of. Learning what you are afraid of requires silence and loud adventure. Many people are afraid of silence and will not take the first step to explore their fears in silent introspection because of this. Some of the most frightening experiences can be gleamed from introspection, beginning with pondering our fears.

Pain and fear are not necessarily undesirable, at least in their initial reward of learning self-preservation. One learns from a little pain and fright so that one is not burned constantly and so that one doesn't fall down a deep pit while looking at flowers. Don't fall, don't burn, but face the fears, that are False Evidence Appearing Real holding you down and preventing you from doing, being and becoming or often just asking a question or saying something. Some of our fears protect us from demise, but we're complex and occasionally obsessive compulsive, with so many experiences that may or may not be relevant, but become relevant to our thinking, and instead of protecting us prevent us. Fear is the most the most influential of feelings and mostly based on false evidence from past experiences and interpretations of past experiences.

Fear is a heavy weight and hindrance, lose it and one gains sight and greater ability to discern for emotions precede thought. Guilt, though normally slighted by fear, is also an immense emotional hindrance and runs second to fear. The two emotions result in negative hate and ignorance and hindrance of potential. See the opportunity in facing fears to develop and open up.

74. Consider what people did and learned in the past. Today our interaction with nature and more than that our interaction with one another individually and collectively is mechanized and limited. People once learned how to grow things, it being honorable

to do so. People once learned how to think things through so as to refine growth, so as to be able on their own without the World Wide Web.

Consider that people once figured the ability to grow plants and raise animals was the barest minimum knowledge. Of course some were better at it than others, but practically everyone grew plants and raised animals. Farming as complex as it is was once considered the barest minimum knowledge you could have to survive in the world, while medicine and healing were considered the pinnacle knowledge one could possibly attain.

Consider the Trivium of grammar, logic and rhetoric. These were considered simple primary instruction at university since the Renaissance. Only on learning language, valid thinking and thought presentation could a student move on to the study the Quadrivium; arithmetic, astronomy, geometry and music. And only after at least gaining a preliminary understanding of these subjects could the student move on to study medicine for instance.

People like Benjamin Franklin who was an inventor, scholar, author and politician were likely able to accomplish so many different things because of a quality education. Quality education doesn't just fill the vessel, quality education creates a better vessel. Today there is more information available to us yet our vessels frequently leak and can only hold so much. See if you, with all the information at your fingertips, can come up with a new concept that can withstand the test of validity through the Trivium.

75. Liberate minds. The most powerful thing you can do is teach someone something so they can help themselves. The most unproductive thing you can do is withhold teaching and information for yourself. Helping someone out with food or money can sustain them for a time, but assisting people with information they can use to earn money for food or information to better themselves in some way is the most helpful thing you can do.

Elephants in Africa traverse the land and the elder ones show the younger ones the way. When an elder elephant dies the younger ones often do not know where to go. The smartest animals, like humans and elephants, need the greatest assistance from their elders and those in the know. It requires true mastery to copy and learn, to observe the nuances and understand the form and function of tension and relaxation takes true mastery. Anyone however can be fooled into following a false master or false guide. Choose whom you learn from wisely.

76. Lose your ego, lose yourself and be the idea. Be a transmitter of an idea greater than yourself. Be part of a process greater than yourself. But don't go around thinking how great you are. God or universal consciousness or chi or prana will work through you when you lose your ego. No matter if you are approaching subjects of athletic or artistic matters when you lose your ego you gain clarity and connection with things greater than yourself.

Remember to stay humble, but never go around thinking the thought, an effective albeit highly negative mantra, "there is nothing I can do about it." Nothing will weaken you more in the long run though it might be comforting at the time when facing an out of control problem. Our thoughts are like programming and often it is as simple as programming ourselves to be who we want to be; ourselves.

Only when you lose your ego can you truly be yourself for all the distractions and fears of the ego eat up your true being like society eats away at individuality. When you lose your ego you can truly be creative unhindered by the distractions and fears that society has placed on us and that we place on ourselves. When the ego loses control meditative practice becomes valuable. And ultimately when the ego isn't controlling and interfering with your relaxed mind state, constantly blasting its own impulses and projections, your mind becomes more open to understanding whether through tangible observation or intangible access to the Akashic field. In order to know let go of your ego.

Sometimes, whenever possible just forget about the labels you've adopted about who you are, forget about who others think you are and how others think you are and just be. Take a sabbatical of sorts whenever possible whether for an hour or a day or more and just be. And remember as you go that everyone around you is your neighbor sharing the same time and place. Such a practice can help disconnect the control the ego has.

77. Eliminate unnecessary wants and you eliminate unnecessary suffering. Buddhism is perhaps the most developed theology in the sense that it boils down the root of suffering and seeks to alleviate it. Your suffering comes from wanting, release the want and you release the suffering for the lack of it. Live simply. Many theorize that one can live in abundance or poverty simply based on your perspective of wants and needs.

Realize the difference 0 and 1, between nothing and something, between no one and someone. People spend so much of their time pursuing more that they often find they have run out of time in the process of acquiring more stuff. The difference between having nothing and having something is a vast canyon, whereas the difference between having enough and more than enough is a matter of a hop, skip and jump.

The best meals are those after a period of going without or a period of hard work. The best nights rest occurs after the same. The best meal and best rest does not pertain to the best chef or best mattress. The things which people are most attached are often the most trivial. Truly valuable things are never possessed, never held by the hand to please the mind, but held in the mind to please through the hand. Knowledge and wisdom are valuable, not possessions. Knowing internal arts such as chi gung, yoga and meditation is worth more than any car or clothing. Such knowledge cannot be taken from you and can always be shared with others.

"The conscious and intelligent manipulation of the organized habits and opinions of the masses is an important element in democratic society. Those who manipulate this unseen mechanism of society constitute an invisible government which is the true ruling power..." ~Edward Bernays

78. Trust yourself. And doubt every other thing until it cannot be doubted anymore. Natural conditions and societal conditions are entirely different circumstances. Do not doubt the sun, just doubt everything in the kingdom. When you can doubt the presentation of situations you can surpass the current dynamic of belief, beliefs which often limit true perceptions by clouding them with amorphous and unfounded sense of this or that. Trust yourself and the universal creator, but do not trust the beliefs of others. Trust yourself and thrust off all the guilt that has been put on you unjustly. Make yourself innocent and open up that trust. Trust yourself, your center, your heart

and your tree, but do not trust your beliefs for they are as the leaves of the trees, subject to falling off and likely to blow around in the airy breezes of societal impulses crowding the view.

To fully trust yourself you must go through some doubt and shed yourself of the beliefs that have grown on you. Sometimes people can't see the forest through the trees because of the beliefs blowing around. Shed your beliefs about situations and circumstances which have no deep roots aside from preconceptions and sensations which have grown on you. Shed your beliefs until you are rooted. Shed what people believe you to be and the beliefs that have fallen on you about yourself and the world outside of you.

Do not have imaginary negative conversations with imaginary people about imaginary confrontations. If you find yourself replaying imaginary negativity you are engulfed in beliefs, your sight is clouded by flying leaves.

In my experience the combination of dedication to daily practice and an innocence leads to great awakening. If one is not both dedicated and innocent one cannot ascend the tree. Meditators and martial artists alike often speak of being like a newborn. Be like a newborn, without prior belief structures that hold down an enhanced mind. To be innocent one must be like a newborn, in compassionate mind state, but really just open and of nothing, or no sense, not of nonsense, but more like in no sense. Innocents are in immersed in no sense. They are immersed in their true nature, which enabling true capability. No saints would ever be angry for any infraction because of dedication to practice and being in no sense. When freed of the senses and/or sense of belief we are capable of enhanced intuition and understanding.

"No doubt, no awakening. Little doubt, little awakening. Great doubt, great awakening." ~Zen Koan

"At the bottom of great doubt lies great awakening. If you doubt fully, you will awaken fully." ~Hakuin Ekaku

"I must be willing to give up what I am in order to become what I will be." ~Albert Einstein

79. Present perseverance and endurance is worth more than prowess and excellence as far as it concerns scholarly commitment or athletic performance. Everything takes time to learn and requires practice and commitment. Those who are proficient were not born that way. Often those who are the best and brightest faced similar failures as others more repetitively. We are all born capable of being in The Zone. Everyone can climb the mountain of being in The Zone. People who are higher up on the mountain simply have committed to climbing there.

"It's not that I'm so smart; it's just that I stay with problems longer." ~Albert Einstein

80. Don't worry. One can face problems without worrying. If one does worry there are basically two results of worry or stress; more worry, stress and wear on the self that degrades performance or alternatively taking positive action to alleviate the problem causing the stress. Remember to pay attention to your breath and change it if there is an unsolvable complexity causing worry and wear. Be mindful of breath and change it to change how the stress. The more stressed one becomes the shallower, more erratic and quicker one's breath becomes. Slow, steady, deep, and aware breath results in reduced stress and relaxation.

Sometimes when we let go of trying to manipulate the outer universe we can better influence it. It is a counterintuitive trick that when you let go, you find you don't need to hold on. When things are of control, it is as if we can do nothing and we are swayed. We can only really control our emotions, thoughts, actions and speech. Basically all else is out of our control, until that is we let go. Understanding what we control leads to yielding any grip on absurdity leading to increased clarity.

"Tension is who you think you should be. Relaxation is who you are." ~Chinese Proverb

81. Celebrate mantras that you identify with and even positive affirmation that you create from your identity. The first rule of repeating mantras or positive affirmations is to never state "I want..." If you are to do the meditation and unconsciously employ the affirmation of "I want..." one will only be in want. Whatever it is you may want one must employ the "I am..." The intent must be there truly, whether you are aware of it

or not. Repetition of the positive intention or affirmation is crucial to its effectiveness. Create your own mantra to experiment with effectiveness. The ancients of course practiced mantra repetition 108 times. 100 times was seen as complete and 8 more were added to correct any errors.

The following are some mantras I use occasionally: "Two to make it true." "There is nothing to it but to do it." "I am love." "I trust." "I am the one." "I am loved and I am loving." "I am the...(insert your focus of actualization)" "I am a bowl, not a chair."

The last quote is a martial and internal arts understanding. This mantra of actualization is initially riddle-like, but actually holds deep meaning. The bowl symbolizes being a container of energy, the bowl symbolizes an activated dantien. The dantien is an energy point just below the navel where it is believed most all action originates. The chair of course represents a space for inactive chi. The (lower) dantien, in tai chi and chi gung, is the same in understanding as the third chakra in yoga systems.

When we are upset we find ourselves literally chanting to ourselves of what upsets us. When we are lonely we might say something like, 'I am the loneliest person I know.' Or 'I am ugly.' We tell ourselves things which aren't true and if anything exaggerate or perpetuate the problem and take up our time keeping our mind state at the same rate. Instead shift your thinking, 'I am the most loved and loving person I know.' Or, 'I am beautiful.'

So much of our time is spent dwelling in pause, conceptualizing something like, 'I have to wait until this and then I'll begin that.' Or, 'when this happens then I'll be happy.' Do not meditate on 'waiting for them' mantras, for the timing is up to you. Instead flip it, 'I am happy and this is happening.' Instead of waiting be loved and loving now. Try repeating your mantra to yourself 108 times.

82. Learn and practice utilization of the tai chi principle of relaxation during your activities whatever they may be. The tai chi principle of relaxation describes the mindset and body-set of being in The Zone. Mastery of an activity and being in The Zone results in effortless performance. This effortless perfection of being in The Zone is what is meant by relaxation in tai chi.

Snowboarding and skiing illustrate the concept perfectly, for in few other circumstances does body and mind positioning make all the difference every second. The slightest error, the minutest mismanagement of the balance of mind and body means all the difference between a successful turn and a high speed tumble. As with any activity, sport or otherwise, one has to strike a balance between form and function or method and style. Imagine this as one line with form on one side and function on the other. One also has to develop a balanced approach to the matter via managing tense and limp positioning. Imagine this as another line intersecting the first line. Imagine balancing the horizontal line of form and function and balancing the vertical line of tense and limp and being in the middle of that intersection. That midpoint of relaxation and alignment is The Zone.

A similar cross reference model can be used to understand and maintain a relaxed heart and mind state. Imagine that your individual consciousness is vertical. The consciousness of others, whether mass consciousness of a great collective, or small group or other individual relates with our individual consciousness horizontally. If you're are steady and rooted vertically then imbalanced or upsetting outside influences will be less likely to throw you off. You will be above it. The higher our vibration and the more rooted we are the less likely outside influences will shake us.

Practice being stoic or at least having a poker face where one appears stoic, mostly unmoved by pleasure and pain. Practice not flinching and practice turning your flinch into an appropriate response. When you flinch, you throw yourself off from being jumpy, when turn the power of the flinch into a response, you save yourself.

83. Realize the ebb and flow of life reflected in the microcosm and the macrocosm. The individual is a reflection of the universal and connected to the universe. We are a reflection of universal consciousness. We are made up of the stardust of 108 elements animated by will, love, wisdom correlating to the fixed, mutable and cardinal signs of astrology. These ideas are numerically depicted using 108 or 801 depending on one's approach, as for instance there is infinite wisdom of oneness. We are the microcosmic individual reflections of the universal, just as the numbers, 1, 0, 8 are the only numbers that are the same whether viewed directly or in a reflection.

The microcosm is reflective of the macrocosm through 108. The planet weaves around the Sun via distances and diameters divisible by 108 and 108 is reflective in our very breath and our meridians. Planetary sacredly aligned constructions contains 108 factors as well. Stonehenge is 108 feet in diameter. This alone might be perchance, but it sits in a bigger series of symbolic stonework that is a 1,082 feet diameter circle in which is also the layout for a building 108 feet long. All three measurements point to the fact that the integration of 108 is no coincidence. Through 108, the universal system, the planetary system and the individual make connection.

Learn about what are called the microcosmic and macrocosmic orbits. These Taoist chi gung meditation practices are said to enable transmutation of inner and universal energy and lead to immortality. The theory behind the meditation is that everyone has an energy line in the front going downwards. And everyone has an energy line in the back going upwards. Invigorating the polarized energy into a smooth flow balances and empower individuals.

The microcosmic orbit and macrocosmic meditations expand on this idea. One circulates energy in one way, the other in a larger orbit. Each is done by sitting in lotus position or on the edge of a firm chair with the back unsupported and straight. Breathe from your dantien deeply, slowly and steadily. Expand your abdomen on inhalation and contract on inhalation. You can try the opposite as well; contracting the abdomen on inhalation and expanding on exhalation. Just concentrating on your breath in this way calms the body and reduces the impact of stressors, allowing the body to regain balance. Imagine energy orbiting down the front from the crown of the head and up the from the sacrum.

The chi gung North Star meditation is used to connect our individual microcosm with the universal macrocosm. Imagine a connection with the stillness of the North Star with the stillness of the light of the inner self. Imagine connecting the celestial with the individual, the heavenly and the earthly, through your crown and spine. The North Star guides travelers physically and is said to guide spiritual travelers as well and be the portal to universal energy. Imagine you are a conduit of consciousness between heaven and earth, giving and receiving energy. Many other meditations describe similar universal energy coming down the back from the crown intersecting with mother earth energy coming up the feet and down/out the tailbone in dual cycles.

These five thousand year old meditations are magical and enlightening way to correlate the micro and macro, self with universe. One should seek instruction for these meditations. The energy lines involved in these meditations can on one level be equated to the parasympathetic and sympathetic aspects of the nervous system. The parasympathetic part of the nervous system acts automatically and is responsible for glandular activity, such as saliva production, digestion and defecation, unconscious thought. While the sympathetic reacts to input and conscious thought and is responsible for the organs and reactions to sensations and stressors. The two main aspects of the nervous system mostly counterbalance each other. The microcosmic flow meditation the parasympathetic system is said to have "craniosacral outflow" and the sympathetic nervous system, said to have "thoracolumbar outflow." In meditation we calm the sympathetic and enable the parasympathetic to a higher point of balance.

Life has its ups and downs, its growth and collapse, its spiraling, pulsing, rising and tumbling. Life is elation flowed by stagnation, it is mundane intermingled with insane and if one is capable of realizing that situations sway, that for every downturn there is an upturn you will be better able to cope and continue. In the cold the most warming thought is that it will soon be warm again.

What doesn't kill you makes you stronger. Adversity is the fire which transforms ore to iron. One can react positively or negatively to adversity and downward spirals, realization that change is always ahead and that adversity hones and comfort and inspire.

"If you're going through hell, keep going." ~Winston Churchill

84. Be flexible and remember that to be completely flexible one must maintain the ability to be rigid. Be persistent and don't let negative people get inside your head. Hold onto your ideas. Don't let people, authorities, family, friends, opponents or propagandists infect your thoughts with their ideas which degrade your own thoughts, your positivity, clarity and your inspiration. Many will suggest you're too young, too old, too much or too little to do or think whatever it is they believe they and you cannot do. Let all who are respectful and courteous in, but don't let the negative people soil your thoughts. Of course, be willing to let go of your ideas so they might grow into more

ascended ones. In contrast you have to be willing to let go in order to grow your ideas so you can stubbornly hold onto.

"I will not let anyone walk through my mind with their dirty feet." ~Gandhi

85. Pick up trash. Whether it's on a walk to a place you've never been before or on familiar ground, at work or at home, pick trash up. You will change the environment and change the perception of those around you. Often, removing trash left behind by irresponsible predecessors and otherwise, is all up to you. Literally, the world needs people to help clean the mess left behind by others. Figuratively, taking responsibility to clean up the trash of others, inspires people to respect you and sometimes take responsibility to help you or others in the same way.

The Tibetan Saint Milarepa who is likely represents the origination of the clichéd wise man on the mountain was a great meditator, poet and singer. He would use allegorical lessons demonstrating esoteric ideas through comparing nature and the elements to inner emotions, thoughts and occurrences. Milarepa manifested change through inner work and was always focused on our integration with and the similarities with man and the environment. You reflect your surroundings and your surroundings reflect you.

Thomas Edison said, "Five percent of the people think, ten percent think they think and eighty five percent would rather die than think." When we are not thinking we will literally kill ourselves and allow ourselves to be enslaved in a destroyed environment. Take care of self and surroundings and realize the micro reflects and projects the macro. Think about your thinking in order to elevate your thinking.

86. Take time for introspection and inspection. Find the flaws within your thinking and within your psyche and eject them. Most everyone has some you might have many, find them and eject them. If you do not face your flaws they will linger. Carl Jung described four ways in which one can deal with the shadow, representing the unknown aspects of our own unconscious. One can act in denial, projection, integration or transmutation of the shadow of our individual consciousness as well as the shadows of mass consciousness. In relationships there are directly recognizable causations in the interplay. There are also the unknowns or shadows which are just as causational as the

realized interaction. One can live in denial of the world. One can live projecting what one experiences. One can integrate one's experiences to better make accommodations for self. The fourth reaction is the most developed, transmutation of one's experiences to better totality.

Learn your limits -in order to surpass them. No one begins proficient. As far as snowboarding goes as a skill I went from total inability, to high speed edge catching scorpions to my face (if you are unaware what a scorpion is, they are worse than they sound) to edge catching off of a cornice –into a front flop. The next time I approached the cornice with speed and determined focus I took the accidental gracelessness and transformed my flight into purposeful grace. My scorpion turned into a front flop and then a front flip. Later when I tried to learn how to do a frontside rodeo which is essential a backflip and a 180 or an inverted 540 I practiced my frontside 180, frontside 540 and backflips and I can honestly say I stomped my first frontside rodeo I attempted like I knew exactly what I was doing. I crashed and scrubbed out on dozens of other frontside rodeo attempts, but I stomped the first one with fogged goggles and all because I worked my way up to it. Know you limits so that you can learn how to take what you do know and transform it into new things that were once unknown.

87. Increase your vocabulary. I say so not because I'm a writer, but more as one interested in politics and people. Language is a map and the more you know the more you are able to understand the terrain of society. Our thinking is limited and enhanced by the quality the language we speak and the vocabulary we have.

Don't gossip. Friends speak more with than they talk about. Don't insinuate or suggest or reduce conversation with such exchanges even if that's how others converse. Be blunt and be positive when you speak instead of slurring conversation with subtle negativity. Be quiet when people on subjects of little consequence to be know for the quality of your words instead of the quantity of them. If you spend your time thinking and speaking about things of little consequence you will come to new insights about things of little consequence. Instead look at the big picture to come up with great insights. Then when you do speak, people will listen. And when others speak you will be better understand truly where they are coming from.

Remember that your word is sacred. What you speak you become. Remember to at least respect if not revere your words and the words of others too. Revere words only if they qualify as compassionate and when they are not, usually those concerned with things of little consequence will be silent. This is when it's most important to speak in nuanced compassionate tone.

88. Accept your intuition. The following information has helped me better understand my intuition. In a sense the information and understanding helped me transform blind random moments of intuition, akin to being in the dark with a dim flickering, into equally blind and random moments of brighter flashes and flickers. I don't mean to suggest I have psychic powers or information that would give others psychic powers, only that it is something I have questioned and looked to understand. The information I found has allowed me to communicate how I saw the flashes in the dark and dare I say helped me build my own sight to better see during the flickers.

All information can be broken down into four parts. Human mythology and the mythology of the mind can be understood literally, allegorically, comparatively and secretively. There is also the tangible and reflections of the tangible and the intangible and reflections of the intangible. Similarly there is the known knowns, known unknowns, unknown unknowns and unknown knowns. The unknown knowns are the most fantastic and of course shifting your perspective can shift the category the information resides. Information might be noted by four ways too; physically, mentally, spiritually or naturally. Physically could be through our funny bone, mentally through emotional twitch, spiritually could be a whisper that is you, but not you and naturally can be the call at a certain time or outside world revealing things to you.

The Zohar describes four ways to interpret theology and theosophy in the four PaRDeS. This idea can be applied to other subjects as well. There is literal, allegorical, comparative and secretive interpretation of text and life. The Four PaRDeS of theology extrapolated as a lens to view society is layered firstly by surface understanding, our individual senses. The secondary more elaborate layer of understanding society arrives in the teachings of others. Thirdly is a combination of collective learning and our own experience used comparatively. Lastly is the intuitive approach where one cannot explain exactly how one reaches an answer, but the answer is correct. All theology or theosophy points the intuitive power inside individuals and all of processes to reach that point. Just as one can always turn unknowns to knowns one can also turn shadows into recognized understandings of individual consciousness and mass consciousness.

Practicing cloudbursting is a good way to start refining the psychic abilities of manifesting. Focus and pushing or pulling the vaporous cloud into simple formations you decide on. When cloudbursting, consciously transforming clouds or when applying and receiving energy in capacity it is most effective to relax one side of your body and and apply tension to the other side. Make one palm active and the other is passive. Imagine energy emanating from the passive palm. Imagining and positioning oneself in this manner, with passive and active sides to your body results in negative and positive electromagnetic flow. Think of having an active left side and passive right, then switch. Also think about passive right leg, passive left arm with active right leg and active right arm and then switch.

Imagine space at its very essence. All space is actually filled up with and made up by particles. Everything you touch is actually made of particles bouncing together and off of each other temporarily held together at different vibrational levels. Imagine that you are made of billions of particles put together at a frequency of consciousness. Imagine that there are billions of particles around you interacting with you, bouncing off of you and being absorbed by you and around these billions of particles are just more particles until the cloud or whatever. Imagine if you can have an effect on just a few particles and these particles begin an chain reaction eventually you have set billions of particles in motion.

Whenever seeking the assistance of the collective or universal consciousness to allow you to apply your force onto the universe and alter a particle or cloud or anything beyond that, one's intent must be positive and one must ask for permission. The universal consciousness is a wild character and if one ever thinks one is in control one will in that moment be bucked. Always be graceful and appreciative of any flicker or glimpse or allowance of a push and pull of a particle and openly reveal intention for permission.

Practice listening to your intuition so far as to listen for intuitive ideas and then practice acting on them. Don't do anything rash however because you will experience many conjurations and projections in taking such course to learn intuition. The same way as one has to learn proper form for a sport one has to learn proper form for intuitive practices. And in the same way one becomes more capable or more knowledgeable the more one practices a sport or studies a subject one will become more intuitive the more one opens oneself to learning and practicing it. Learn to distinguish your own projections with true reflections.

Practice burning a tear. This meditative practice is done using a candle or any point in front of one's field of view. Sit or stand and breathe meditatively. Keep your eyes open. Do not blink until a tear is burned out of each eye. Meditate on seeing differently during this.

Meditate in mirrored rooms or looking in a mirror with your eyes open.

Meditate seeing a chalkboard or piece of paper. Ask a question and imagine writing the answer.

Meditate on your third eye. Meditate and relax. After you are relaxed focus on looking at your third eye with your eyelids closed and focus you're your chi there too. Take about 108 breaths. Then relax your eyes. Then open them and remain meditative with your eyes open for a few minutes.

Meditate on darkness. Ask yes or no questions and imagine green or red lights going off to represent yes or no answers.

Use a deck of cards to first guess color, then suit, then color and face card, then specific card. Guess who is calling you. Think of a person and see if they call you. Guess the story behind newspaper photos.

When seeking to gain psychic insight or intuitive glimpses try practicing Buddhist breath. On inhalation let your abdomen expand and push out. On exhalation relax and return to normal. Imagine being receptive and opening up.

Intuition comes in many forms. When the heart and mind are connected, that is when our thoughts and emotions are balanced as well as our inner senses and outer senses and when we are more likely to obtain hints of great obscurity.

Do not let your thoughts override your emotions or vice-versa. One's heart/mind state or one's perspective controls how well one feels. We control how we feel, but more importantly how we feel controls us. How we feel can blatantly and/or subtly influence others too. So lose stress, loosen up and look around. In order to truly be open to universal consciousness, the Akashic field, the holy spirit, inner intuition or whatever one wants to call this energy one has to be completely open. In order to be completely open or approach such openness we have to practice loving kindness. There are many ways to do this, however generally speaking one must let go of hate and jealousy and all negative heart/mind states. If you can be open with the person who most irritated you or angered you, you can be open to universal consciousness, more intuitive.

"The intuitive mind is a sacred gift and the rational mind its faithful servant. We have created a society that honors the servant and has forgotten the gift." ~Albert Einstein

89. Fast every once in a while. Fasting for a day or so and only consuming water is a great way to cleanse and provide rest to the digestive system, and basic time for the body to balance and heal itself. Fasting with the inclusion of fresh organic lemon juice, maple syrup and cayenne can be beneficial especially when fasting for longer periods than a day.

90. Learn about Wu Wei. This Taoist idea means the action of non-action. Wu Wei is being in The Zone. It is performing great and graceful feats effortlessly. It is living and acting in conjunction with the rhythm of nature and relations with other beings. Wu Wei, performing action in non-action and being in The Zone is not exactly going with the flow, Wu Wei and being in The Zone is more specifically flowing with the flow. Learning and practicing skill is important, but to be true master one has to let go of structure and be without form, letting go being one way or another and just being.

The similar Zen idea of Mushin or Mushin No Shin means mind without mind in Japanese. This state, gained through learning and practice is one where the mind and heart, one's thoughts and emotions are open and flowing instead of being held static on a thought or emotion. This state in martial arts, or snowboarding or any activity is being in the moment so that one's training and experience allows you to flow with your opponent or the elements. In life this state is applicable the same understandable via the idea of not just going with the flow, but flowing with the flow. Mushin is egoless, fearless and more over thoughtless and emotionless.

The following quotes are all from Bruce Lee:

"Art reaches its greatest peak when devoid of self-consciousness. Freedom discovers man the moment he loses concern over what impression he is making or about to make."

"All fixed set patterns are incapable of adaptability or pliability. The truth is outside of all fixed patterns."

"Using no way as way, using no limitation as limitation."

"Obey the principles without being bound by them."

"The consciousness of self is the greatest hindrance to the proper execution of all physical action."

91. Learn how to focus. Focus can be allegorically illustrated in both looking at and exploring the grains of sand at your feet and by scanning and observing the massive horizon. Before you can be in a state of Wu Wei or Mushin you have to practice mindful attention to the minute details in everything. You have to train to the point where you critique each little muscle movement or each inflection of thought. Meditate your focus on your training to un-train before becoming able to do without doing, fight without fighting. Focus on your training for whatever pursuit and remember that all the benefits of self-development and individuation crossover, through integration, to benefit mind, body, spirit and surroundings.

Raja Yoga or simply yoga holds presents an eightfold path toward becoming. One must become balanced and follow attentive procedure before one can let go and find the bliss of mind no mind. First there is self-restraint, next is commitment and devotion, thirdly is integration of the mind and body through activity, then integration of mind and body through regulation of breath, then withdrawal of the senses from traditional perception, followed by concentration, meditation and the quiet state of blissful awareness.

Meditation on the Hindu idea of Brahman and Atman can assist one in developing focus. Brahman is all things as one, the entire universe, the complete macrocosm. Atman is the smallest point of individual consciousness within a living being, the microcosm. During meditation imagine compressing, focusing your very own individual consciousness into a single point. Hold your breath, count to 21, and tense all your muscles and sinews of your whole body. Imagine your consciousness come together in the very center of your head into one point, one point of light if it suits you. Observe the single point of self and nothing else. For Brahman observe the infinite with nothing missing as 1. When one can observe and focus on Brahman and Atman focusing on all else becomes easier. To better focus, whether in meditation or an activity of any sort, think of 108; let there be nothing, 0, between the oneness of your very singularity and infinity.

92. Live in tune with your surroundings and seek to understand your surroundings. Only then can we change our surroundings. This might mean practicing seasonal tradition involving shopping locally or practicing seasonal specific sports. It can expand into consideration of your environment rather than consideration of profit or quick comfort before all else. In nature things happen for a reason.

Ever since the Big Bang things have been reacting. Here on Earth is no different. The birds squawk in reaction to a deer approaching, the deer is approaching because there are raspberries in bloom, the raspberries are in bloom because it's summer, it's summer because we revolving around the sun, the sun burns because it's made of radioactive material from the Big Bang. If the Big Bang is too far back to reach, or if the Big Bang isn't applicable enough for you, pick another point in creation. Understanding that people and all life are just reacting to things allows you to better gauge what is happening and better gauge what might happen.

Listen to the birds. Be aware of the waste you produce and what happens to it. Life on Earth is a miracle. Recognize the miracle you are and the miracle all of others and all else is. Recognize hints of miraculous, take miraculous hints, warnings and opportunities.

Radionuclides, industrial or militaristic sourced radiation, is difficult to quantify and measure and impossible to see. The conundrum of nuclear experimentation is so vast and deep of an alteration most people will not consider it entirely and many have not considered it at all. When people begin to break down because they learn about the unsettling horrors and consequences of nuclear experimentation I like to point out the formula for activist as well as magical transformation.

108 illustrates the magical and activist construct for change. 1 is for acceptance. We cannot change anything unless we understand and accept reality. 0 is for integration. We cannot change anything until we integrate reality, combining everything until it just is, until there is no negative or positive just the mix if you will. 8 is for the transmutation. Only after acceptance and integration can we change reality in infinite ways. If we did not understand it, or integrate the entirety of it, change does not progress as well as it could otherwise.

We must accept the reality of any number of situations, including environmental destruction before transmuting it. Many times when I reveal the complexity of nuclear experimentation to people they become disappointed in the message, the deliverer of the message and are just overwhelmed. In other words they do not get past the acceptance phase toward change. It is an absolutely overwhelming subject, however humanity manifested it appearance and we can also manifest its disintegration. We have to unite against nuclear experimentation or we will be united in our own dissolution, our own degradation and death.

This is the biggest problem addressing the polluted and bereft environment of the Netherworld Oligarchy, that the majority refuses to accept reality. We have to communicate for radiation knows no borders, it cares for no culture or ideal, it causes deformation of offspring if it does not kill you. Nuclear experimentation is the ultimate abhorrence to all Earth beings.

The integration phase is allegorically akin to the witches throwing in sacred herbs as well as crow's feet and snake heads into the cauldron. Everything has to be mixed in, everyone has to be forgiven and we have to form together where there is no negative and no positive, just the brew. We have to forgive each other and integrate all of our potentiation. Integration stirs the mix and unless there is no outright absolutely unforgivable and despicable evil, everything is integrated.

In order to transmute we must accept and integrate. The transmutation, true change or change in truth rather, comes from manifestation in openness, without obfuscation, without discernment for positive and negative and forgiven and unforgiven. This lacking of close mindedness allows for positive flow and positive alteration. When revenge or close mindedness clouds our decision making and our potentiation we are less able to transmute in a truly positive manner.

1/Acceptance, 0/Integration 8/Transmutation. In the case of nuclear experimentation it is in fact so dastardly, so infinitely and obviously negative to so many generations and biological systems it can in fact incite unity. Nuclear experimentation can unite us all politically, because it does unite use all biologically. We are all under biological attack by the industrial and militaristic soot of oligarchical energy systems of our own design, of our own manifestation. Now we have to change our approach and manifest a true solution to the problems of our own design. The solution is in activist transmutation, illustrated using the magical formula of 108. And the next time someone calls you negative because you are raising awareness of the extent of the problem share this formula with them. Transmutation begins with understanding.

93. Maintain youthful exuberant curiosity. Just thinking about this alleviates burden and rigidity. Cultivation of open childlike curiosity is one of the most important ways to maintain youth and attracts input from others. Assumption of possessing the highest knowledge closes you off and repels others. Everything begins in the mind. Thinking openly and curiously enables you to learn about the wonders of the universe and results in character of openness instead of always labeling and judging and even prejudging. The worst thing one can do is become an unquestioning professional who doesn't need to learn more. This means that you are not excelling and that you have peaked. To be excellent, be like the monk inquiring of the child.

94. Seek to be a problem solver. The biggest problem in the world today is environmental destruction. The biggest cause of environmental destruction is the status quo of the oligarchical energy industries. The biggest contributing factor to the destructive status quo of oligarchical energy industries is greed and tolerance of greed. The biggest reinforcement of greed and tolerance of greed is societal traditionalism insisting the system which feed oligarchs is entirely normal. That which allows these reinforcing systems to continue is the fear of change. Change one person and you change the world. Always begin with yourself. The best way to be a peaceful warrior is to take the space of confrontation. In tai chi chuan each step and wave of the hand can be understood as taking the space rather than a kick or punch.

Tai chi chuan is also known as shadowboxing and is one of the highest forms of moving meditations. One aspect of all meditations and especially tai chi is clearing and cleaning our Merkaba or our energy field of negative energies that attack men, or attachments. Tai chi chuan, literally grand ultimate long form or ying yang long form is a highly efficient meditation for clearing as well as simply preparing us for boxing through its shadowboxing. God forbid you actually have to fight someone else at all, tai chi or not, for actually, whether we are aware of the confrontation or not, in life we most often are fighting ourselves in an inner Nietzsche like battle between beastly and saintly, where our ascended humanity has to confront, or box, our descended ego, or our shadow. Meditation and meditative movement allows us to know when to take the space among others by taking back our own space from attachments that attack men - people, often enough through the shadow of our ego.

95. Ask questions and lend money. These two actions are two different practices I realize. And I could have made them into two points, but together they are more memorable as they contain a connection on relationships. I put these two together because in social circles they are often part of the same application.

As a general rule people are made uncomfortable by intense questioning of serious situations for most people are trained to not question and not to answer. Sometimes questions will lead to direct answers and sometimes answers to unasked questions. Asking questions about subjects you know about or are ignorant of leads to potential understanding of the subject and definite understanding of those around you. For instance they may know what you know, they may or may not bother to teach you what they know, they may lie about what they know, they may judge you for apparently not knowing or they may presume they know something when they do not. Inquire frivolously and seriously, but begin with the frivolous and work your way to the serious. Frequently if you inquire of the frivolous first you might receive information pertaining to the serious before asking. Frequently frivolous questions will lead to more open and serious answers.

Question your friends and family and most importantly question authority. Of course questioning authority is the most empowering research and often a question can be as rattling as the eventual answer. Questioning is supreme to maintaining a positive, open outlook and to developing and maintaining the quality of one's surroundings.

If you are in a debate with yourself about a decision to be made or in a debate with another person about anything consider the Socratic Dialectic. Be perceptive and question the foundation of all sides of the debate. If debating another person ask questions so that their own answers disprove them. If debating yourself ask questions in the same way so that you can reach the best answer or approach.

As further test and practice of intuitive powers, look people in the eye when you ask them questions. Perhaps you will only develop a keen sense of facial expressions revelatory to true thought/feeling behind the eyes, but the eye truly is a window to the soul and a lens to see out from and into. You will also let people know that you are looking into their eyes –for the truth and they will be less likely to lie to you in the future, of course this will go unsaid 99% of the time.

Lending money requires an openness and non-judgmental attitude obtainable through questioning. The exchange can also be as revelatory of individual character as answers to questions. Don't break the bank for just anyone, don't enable someone's negative behavior, but lending small amounts of money to friends and family can help them and also reveal their character.

"If you have money, do not lend it at interest, but give it to one from whom you will not get it back." ~Gospel of Thomas, 95

96. Respect whomever you disagree with. And don't be afraid to tell them or anybody why you disagree. Communication leads to education. Respectful disagreement will lead to respectful communication. Do not let political correctness restrict your communication or worse your thinking. Often the subjects which are the most taboo are most revelatory of what is really going on. You have to stand up and say something or whomever is riding your back will remain there. You have to say something to finish something and start something. Sometimes respectful truth can be enough to start discussion for the things which most require discussion, which are the most taboo, are often the most outrageous and repulsive things making it so all you have to do is get the information out there and then people will see the understanding in your disagreement. Such is nuclear experimentation, such is war, such is all the pollution from the runoff of our greed seen, smelled and tasted globally. Very little exaggeration and very few expletives are required to describe the horrible negativity resulting in cancers and

permanent negative alteration of the DNA of all life. Our pollution and our lifestyle are corrupt and killing us.

97. Make and hold onto your team. No matter how you put yourself out there by yourself, have a team, whether family or friends to fall back on and to lean on for support. There is nothing more valuable than being part of a likeminded group except perhaps being part of a likeminded group who seek to help each other and benefit their surroundings. Few things can be so supportive and empowering as a solid group of family or friends and few things are so rewarding as being there for such a group.

98. Be a righteous rebel. Sometimes respectful and courteous exchange of information is not enough. Sometimes the system and all your peers stand against you and what you know to be true and more over absolutely righteous and in opposition of evil. Sometimes you have to be a rule breaker and table tosser for sometimes this is needed to better the world. This is why there are civil disobedience laws on the books. This is why heroes like Nelson Mandela are often thrown into prison. Legality is often not based on morality and often is based on maintaining an oligarchy. Such persistent systemization often requires expletives and breaking the rules in a peaceful manner as Jesus, Gandhi, Martin Luther King Jr. and the likes did, as civil disobedience prescribes and inspirational guidance often suggests and demands.

Don't just sit there. If you were meant to just sit there you might have been born with a chair instead of two arms and two legs. You have eyes, ears and a mouth. Use what you have to stand up for yourself and others, because it is in your design, it is your true nature. If you were meant to not consider the conditions outside yourself, of circumstances outside your immediate vicinity, you wouldn't be able to. If you were unable to make a difference concerning conditions within you and outside of you, you wouldn't be reading this.

99. Put more in and take less out. In the past it was noble enough to live according to the philosophy 'put back in what you take out.' Today and evermore, at the rate we're going, because of the toxic runoff from oligarchical collectivism we are forced to endure

environmental degradation and it is important to put more in than we take out. It is important to enliven and enrich instead of simply producing skeletons of decadence. Somehow, anyhow you possibly can, return more and take less. Some legendary cultures believed that it was mentally sick to seek more than you need, especially at the cost of others. Corporate institutions operate in the complete opposite manner, existing n the business model to take more out than they put in. This behavior model tends to trickle down, influencing some individuals to act like corporate institutions. Be an individual, put more in than you take out.

100. In Buddhism there are 108 defilements and delusions of the mind. Practicing meditation and meditative movements heightens awareness and enables one to take control in the metaphysical inner battle for conscious control of self as do realization of and elimination of negative, unkind thinking and being.

The 108 torments or defilements may be something akin to the following: abuse, aggression, ambition, anger, arrogance, baseness, blasphemy calculation, callousness, capriciousness (unaccountable changes of mood or behavior) censoriousness (being severely critical of others), conceitedness, contempt, cruelty, cursing, debasement, deceit, deception, delusion, derision, desire for fame, dipsomania (alcoholism characterized by intermittent bouts of craving), discord, disrespect, disrespectfulness, dissatisfaction, dogmatism, dominance, eagerness for power, effrontery (insolent or impertinent behavior), egoism, enviousness, envy, excessiveness, faithlessness, falseness, furtiveness, gambling, garrulity (tediously talking about trivial matters), gluttony, greed, greed for money grudge, hardheartedness, hatred, haughtiness, high-handedness, hostility, humiliation, hurt, hypocrisy, ignorance, imperiousness (assuming power or authority without justification), imposture (pretending to be someone else in order to deceive), impudence, inattentiveness, indifference, ingratitude, insatiability, insidiousness, intolerance, intransigence (unwilling or refusing to change one's views or to agree about something), irresponsibility, jealousy, know-it-all, lack of comprehension, lecherousness, lying, malignancy, manipulation, masochism, mercilessness, negativity, obsession, obstinacy, obstinacy, oppression, ostentatious, pessimism, prejudice, presumption, pretense, pride, prodigality (spending money or using resources freely and recklessly), quarrelsomeness, rage, rapacity (being aggressively greedy or grasping), ridicule, sadism, sarcasm, seduction, self-denial, self-hatred, sexual lust, shamelessness, stinginess, stubbornness, torment, tyranny, unkindness, unruliness, unyielding, vanity, vindictiveness, violence, violent temper, voluptuousness, wrath.

Avoid and eliminate all the above behaviors. Try to at least regulate and minimize their control over you. Doing the opposite of these 108 behaviors is righteous and virtuous. The foundation of Buddhism is compassion and the Eightfold Path to Enlightenment and then next perhaps the Four Thoughts. The first thought is the precious human body, 1. We are all capable of learning and accomplishing tremendous things. The second thought is that all is temporary, 0. Eventually everything becomes nothing and all mortals perish. The third thought is that everything is made up of karma, 8. Karma comes back around and at you and others often infinitely. The fourth thought is samsara. We are all here in the middle of all this suffering, where, as sentient beings behind every door and behind every smile there is suffering. Samsara is all encompassing condition of life.

The four thoughts lead into the Four Immeasurables, love of self, obviously 1, love for others, love for the happiness of others, both symbolized by 0, though different concepts and love for all things in equanimity, 8. The Four Thoughts and Four Immeasurables enable enlightenment and surpassing such defilements.

101. Better your memory, it betters your brain. Try to remember the names of people you meet. Stating their name on hearing it helps, like 'what do you do ____?' Or 'good to meet you ____.' If one has trouble memorizing names and responsibilities try this: whatever errand or activity requires a mental note, write a small note and place it on a wall or doorway where you will see it. Repeat this dozens of times to the point it is routine and then transform the physical activity into an imaginary one. Imagine writing down a note and placing it on an imaginary space inside you whereupon when you will see the mental note promptly. Try to remember sets of numbers without assistance. Learn something new and then try to remember it, and then remember to test your memory.

Writing with pen and paper was invented in Egypt and China around the same time. An Egyptian tale foretells the potential danger of such an invention. The ancient Egyptians had a story about a magician forefather who invented the written word. The story goes he had an immense fear about the outcome of his invention. Apparently people once thought about the future effects of their inventions, rather than merely the present where we sell them and then see what happens. His fear was that if people were able to write that they would become forgetful and use their mind less, that they may lose more than they gain. Becoming dependent on writing instead of using their brain could ultimately dum down the people. Imagine what the magician forefather would think of today's inventions. Cellphones not only can be used as pen and paper, but all sorts of functions can be installed so one effectively does not have to think at all.

This is a consideration of a form of karma or more simply cause and effect. There are many things to do and many ways to do them. What we aspire to do and how we arrange to do it determines karma. The outcome of the things we invent and manufacture results in a certain direct karma. Today the inventions certainly dilute our brain power, as was feared of writing, but also pollute our surroundings. Try to increase your brain power through simply using your brain more. Activating your memory activates your creativity. Soon you will start to have so many ideas you will find it necessary to carry a pen and paper with you to write down your ideas so you don't forget them, but you can remember more at the same time.

102. Enjoy the trip rather than just looking forward to the destination. This may be a cliché you've heard before, but the reason variations of this phrase have become clichéd is because of the value as a life lesson. Living in this way will enable you to see the green grass around you rather than always ahead, on the other side. If one is always concerned about the destination and not the trip one will less often be in the present. One will tend to look ahead to one's arrival and then, as soon as one reaches the destination, the next destination or the return inhabits one's mind. Enjoying the trip keeps you in the present moment, making all things easier to deal with, and allowing refined, instead of scattered awareness.

103. Never start a fight, but always fight back for yourself and those around you. Be at peace with yourself and those around you, but when someone defies that peace stand up to them. Sometimes one must fight to win and sometimes one need only to fight enough so as to communicate further transgression will come at a cost. Sometimes fighting back does not require physical or verbal confrontation or confrontation on a

level on anyone outside of the in the confrontation would notice. Always be willing to fight to win and fight without care for winning or losing, but just to let transgressors know there will be costs literally. Some people are bad or turn bad and sometimes you have to confront them literally and hopefully allegorically.

.   Stand up for something or someone righteously. When you stand up for the helpless say or when you stand up siding with the righteous you will be empowered. Too many people are apathetic today resulting being and environment lacking invigoration. Apathetic approaches lead to pathetic character, while action based on empathy and sympathy tend to elevate and inspire.

Be a ninja. Ninjas are in tune with their environment, but Ninjas always do the least expected action. In fact it is said that the Ninja based their tactics primarily on the theory that most of what most people did was a predictable reaction based on contemporary training. They trained themselves to counter predictable reactions. It is philosophized that being contrarian is not the same as being creative, but they're close. It is also well recognized that martial arts are not internal arts, but they're close. Martial applications go beyond mere strikes and internal arts do more than develop concentration. Martial and internal arts theories can be applied to life. Be different. Be different through understanding predictable reactions and being on top of the outcome, like a Ninja.

Martial arts frequently refers to the four elements in its teachings; earth, wind, fire and water. In confrontation, literal or allegorical, be like one of the four elements. Be grounded like earth, be light like the wind, be soft and yet forceful like water, be energetic like fire depending on what might work best at the time. Sometimes we need to be rooted like a tree and stand our ground. Sometimes we realize, in whatever way we were incorrect or for whatever reason need to yield a space like the wind or water. Sometimes we need to be intense like fire. Taking a brief moment to contemplate being like one of the elements is an easy, quick way to formulate strategy in interaction or confrontation.

Realize that when someone starts an argument with you it is often because of something going on inside them. And often when someone is hypercritical and argumentative they are doing so because they see something in you that is like them or like how they would want to be. You will find that the loudest people will tell you to shut up, the most obnoxious people will call you rude and those with belief structures which are being disproven will call you delusional or stupid. Always be willing to return an apology even if you don't feel you did anything to warrant an apology. Not apologizing has the potential of making you look small, while apologizing has the potential to elevate all parties.

Never fight walls. There is a way through the wall and often a door. Walls were built to keep in and keep out. And they were also built to be a place where people are stopped.

104. Be patient. The benefits of taking things slowly cannot be overrated. If you have to wait for anyone there is always something more productive you can do other than to think about how horrible it is to be forced to wait. When you have to learn something complicated there is no completion there is just refinement and addition. Contrary to popular opinion, there is no end to the learning and so rushing can ruin.

When we are rushed and attempt to move faster we are more prone to accidents which slow us down. We lend more control to our ego or the trickster and excite the frantic mind causing inattentiveness. Tai chi is practiced slowly so as to refine subtlety and to energizes you a certain way or through a certain layer that works to develop your sinews, micro muscles and organs and creates a subtle energy flow that is difficult to reproduce through other means.

Learning tai chi is extremely difficult and yet just attempting to mimic the movements with someone who knows them is profoundly energizing no matter the level of ability. And never forget that mimicry leads to mastery and individuality. Mimicry is not just the 'monkey see, monkey do' or 'copycat' claims of simplicity. Mimicry is how children learn and adapt and better. And attempting to mimic tai chi, for instance, will show you how difficult proper mimicry is. In some ways only a true master can observe and mimic entirely as well as transform and adopt tai chi or any system in an individual manner. Be patient in observing, learning and practicing anything.

The world today is rushed, so rushed in fact that the moments in which we move in a slow coordinated manner seeking relaxation can stand out like no other and energize like no other. The next time you are hurried see if you can slow down. The next time you are not hurried see how slowly you are able to move while performing a meditative movement like tai chi or while walking or cleaning.

In tai chi chuan theory it is said to practice like a cat. A cat moves slowly and steadily until it lunges. A cat is impeccably balanced so that even when it seems to be off balance in a struggle it is simply relaxing into a new position. Cats sleep in trees, nestled between branches in perfect balancing act absorbing the fluctuations to relax and sleep, though still slightly aware of where it rests. Whether in a tangle or nap, be like a cat, relaxed, ready and rooted.

105. Pay attention to how you speak. Using the words 'mine' and 'my' usually indicates selfish preface to thought. 'I' is like this to a lesser degree. Instead use the words 'the' or 'our.' Pay attention to how you speak in order to better understand how others speak, what they speak about and how they speak about it.

Always speak the same words to people that you would away from them, and always speak more to your friends than about them. These practices help you be impeccable with your word and not slight yourself. We are capable of putting emotions and thoughts into words, speech or text, which have cause and effect as powerful as action, thought or emotion.

Share information and don't keep secrets, but don't start arguments or toss insults. There may be some information of which sharing it will help no one, inconsequential information should be considered as tissue to be tossed. However information that would help or better someone in anyway should be shared. Pass the information through these four gates variously associated with Sufis and Socrates: Are these words true? Are they necessary? Are they beneficial? Are they kind?

Remember that it can require the equivalent time it takes to write a book to gain trust. And more importantly remember that the trust you've gained can be dismantled in the time it takes to read just 1 word. So be wise in what you say and at least occasionally be sparing in how much you say.

106. Listen with your eyes and see with your ears. First was the word, first was sound and vibration. Light is like sound flowing at a higher vibration. Om is perhaps the oldest symbol on the planet and is said to be the primordial sound from which the whole universe was created. Om not so coincidentally is also said at the beginning of

practically every mantra. "In the beginning was the word, and the word was with God." ~John 1:1, in The Bible. Many theosophies clearly point to creation being manifest through a vibration or word of god and physics theorizes the same as this spiritual understanding.

Everything tangible is just coalesced vibration. Everything you perceive as tangible and solid is at its core sound and light, energy vibrations. We are, at a quantum level all one, each perhaps vibrating the sound and light slightly different for the time being. Not only are we originated and manifested through sound, as is entirety, we also can be influenced and healed through sounds and vibrations and light. Likewise there are 'legends' of healers with siddhis (exceptional yogic psychic powers gained through dedication to meditation, powers the results of repetition similar to creating static friction, but over longer periods and on spiritual level) who could simply change the vibration so as to heal and be seers and 'perform miracles' by tapping into the vibration with earthly psychic powers.

432 Hz or cycles per second used to be the accepted convention for the tuning of musical instruments, beginning with 432 for A. 108 multiplied by 4 = 432. 432 also breaks down to 9, of course. 432 squared equals 186,624, the approximate speed of light in MPH, a neat coincidence based on the arbitrary measurement of miles. In 1940, an international standard was set at 440. Research on vibration reveals that even this slight change or modification from what just feels right, to what is easier to set, can have detrimental and disharmonious results leading to sensations of discomfort and even at certain disharmonies, influence of confrontational and erratic behavior.

When we see with our ears and listen with our eyes we don't limit our senses, we expand them and we allow what we imply is impossible to be possible. When we see with our ears, we sense the beginning of situations before they materialize, as if pre-echoes, and when we hear with our eyes, we use our inner eye, inner vision, our entire sightline.

Sometimes it is difficult to quantify from where we sense vibrations, perhaps it is a gut feeling, perhaps something is just ever so slightly off key and because of our previously limited range of perception we can't explain why, but we can still feel what. Openness to vibrations, in all forms, arriving through all doors leads to heightened awareness and more rapid quality response or more distant detection. Being in tune with ourselves and surroundings allows us to better sense vibrations of all sorts, no matter if it is truly negative vibration or simply the difference between consonant and dissonant sounds, unless we are in tune, or in sync with disharmony.

107. Be sensitive. Everyone is sensitive only some people have been dulled to the point they no longer realize they are so, but if a certain button is pushed, sensitized emotions can run high. If one is sensitive without denying it one will be more relaxed in delicate situations, as well as more aware of your surroundings. In many cultures sensitivity is scorned and dullness is promoted, perhaps because it makes one better prepared for delicate situations and to realize what's happening in your surroundings. The difference between being sensitive and being clairvoyant might only be a matter of the quantity of desensitization to life one has experienced. Embrace your sensitivity. Focus on the minute little things around you. Observe what the flowers and spiders do. Observe what you didn't notice initially about birds taking flight and landing.

In tai chi chuan theory there are many subtleties revealed through simple sayings, which hold many layers, the more subtle layers require more sensitive understanding. It is recommended to breathe so softly that one doesn't disturb a goose feather under one's nose. Further it's recommended that one move so attentively that you become aware of the tiniest insect landing on your skin and that even the tiniest fly or mosquito finds no place to land as you're always out of the way. The immediate lesson is that slowing down the breath and paying attention to one's moving posture results in sensitivity to physical surroundings. A more subtle lesson is that practicing heightened awareness of yourself and surroundings develops heightened sensitivity to the metaphysical.

Being aware is just acceptance and training of our sensitivity. Flies have two eyes, each with thousands of eyes within them. Their extraordinary sight and rapid flight makes most movements to swat at or grab them futile. Your fastest swat is a slow fumble to them.

Citrus is acidic and yet when we consume it, it actually makes our systems more alkaline. It is one of many contradictions in form where things are not always what they seem. Most acidic food is causation for acidic systems, but being that citrus benefits us becoming more alkaline and though we function at balanced level, often we need to be more alkaline and less acidic.

This attribute of citrus fruit is like the fruit of tai chi. It is a contradiction in form to think that the slow, attentive and specific movements of tai chi chuan would lead to increased speed of movement and reaction time, but they do. The specific slow articulations originating in the feet, powered by the legs, controlled by the dantien and expressed through the fingers, activate the less dominant side of the body and connect mind body in a very tangible way spurring healthy balance. This mind body link is a new dendrite forest connecting what was once deserted and disconnected neurons, grounding us in the present. Slow movements enhance attention to self and one's surroundings, enhanced attention leads to increased reaction time to the point of having a fly eye reaction and even intuitive understanding. That is to say that not only can one detect movements of those around you just like a fly, as if things are moving in slow motion, but one also gains sensitivity to the surroundings of the situation that can help one avoid figuratively or literally walking down the wrong street, so that one doesn't have to move quickly to get out of the way of falling tree so to speak in the first place.

When we are stressed, we are not grounded and become increasingly erratic and unconscious of ourselves, our surroundings and how we interact with our surroundings. Essentially we get into tangles with literal and figurative falling trees. It is the citrus fruit of tai chi that makes practicing slow, stylized, specific movements enhance the ability to react quicker and in a more appropriate fashion because of enhanced observation due to calm mind state. Practicing slow and attentive movement with the breath develops a fly eye as well as develops technique. The citrus of tai chi for the fly eye can be applied to all situations whether one practices tai chi or not. Move slowly and pay attention so it is easy to be in the right place at the right time.

This idea of enhanced sensitivity training can be practiced anytime, anywhere, despite knowledge of a tai chi form or not. Simply move attentively and breathe slowly and attentively and note to self, 'I am conscious, I am conscious ('of experiencing this or that' as you do whatever it is you're doing, though simply the statement alone 'I am conscious' works well)' continuously or continuously enough to hold the thought.

108. Love. Buddha is known to have pointed to 4 aspects or stages of love related to The Four Immeasurables. Love of self is the first aspect, love of others is the second, love for the happiness of others is third and love of all things in equanimity is the fourth.

Each stage of the following requires the preceding stage of love to be put forth. The Golden Rule is one element, love results from loving others as you would be loved. Just contemplating the four stages of love, love for self, for others, for the happiness of others so they can find enlightenment/dharma and love for all things in equanimity can change things for you and your surroundings.

See the divinity in the relationship between the Sun, Moon and Earth in the ratio of 108. See the divinity of yourself with all of humanity and all living beings, with the entirety of the planet as equally and divinely balanced. 108 can be seen as illustrating love; 1 for unification and acceptance, 0 representing that nothing matters compared to love and 8 representing eternal, immutable compassionate love, no matter what.

It's said that Buddha revealed 84,000 lessons in dharma, or 82,000 lessons and that 2,000 more were later added for a total of 84,000 dharmas, or meditations, antidotes to what are called the 84,000 corruptions. His teachings are divided into four parts, 21,000 teachings on each of the Vinaya, Sutra, Abhidharma, and their combination to counter and cure the gross corruptions on this plane. Buddha's dharma lessons are said to be the antidote to the corruptions, in the same way compassionate love counters confrontation.

There are four types of corruptions, 21,000 of passion ruling, 21,000 of hatred ruling, 21,000 of ignorance and 21,000 of a combination of the three equally. Buddha taught that the way out of suffering is not to cause suffering and that the way to happiness is to choose happiness. Cease allowing passion, hatred and ignorance to rule one's consciousness. Question yourself and others acting in these states. These states of consciousness are reflected in the center of an ancient mandala of reincarnation and the cycle of samsara as the passion of the pig, the hatred of the snake and ignorance of the rooster. They are depicted in a cycle, or reaction, chasing each other's tail. Instead of chasing tails, be compassionate for all, as 1, exclude 0 living beings from your compassion, and be accepting of infinite alternative compassionate form and function, 108.

84,000 is 108 multiplied by 777.7777777777777... 7, 777 and sevens in multitude are symbolic of angelic being, ascension and transmutation of self into a spiritual being with heightened awareness. And perchance, 7+7+7=21. There are 84,000 loving ways to counter 84,000 corruptions, 84,000 compassionate forms to choose from, instead of

84,000 causes for suffering. These 84,000 antidotes also represent solutions to disruptions in the flow of energy in the 84,000 nadis or energy line meridians.

There is always a way to respond lovingly, in angelic being, rather than to react hatefully, in a trained reaction, in accordance to the scripting of another's corrupt play, always a way to respond rather than react. The number 84,000 is more of a metaphor than a specific count of course. It is a metaphor in its angelic numerical relationships perhaps, but more importantly is that it's reflective of the near limitless corruptions on this gross plane and that for each one there is a dharma lesson. For every problem and for every corruption there is a compassionate, caring, wise, solution.

To me this one arithmetic equation is suggestive that not only did the Buddhists have an adept understanding of mathematics, and that the 10 base numerological system may be more optimal, but that both these numbers, 108 and 84,000 are not at all arbitrary, and unlike many numerological systems and understandings and not distractions from spiritual understandings but links to spiritual understandings. Interestingly enough, there are 86,400 seconds in a day, a number close to 84,000. And of course 86,400 divided by 108 equates to the nice and neat result of 800, another instance of interest at least in its neatness.

One of the most popular figures or energies in Tibetan Buddhism is the Green Tara. Tara has 21 aspects, Green Tara being the most frequently praised, and represents the ultimate feminine compassionate energy. There are many ways to connect with Green Tara, one meditation I learned, with accompanying ritual, reveals two main mantras to connect with Green Tara. In summation, there is the heart mantra and the activating mala mantra. It is said when the heart mantra is said 700,000 times and for each thousand that the activating mantra is said three hundred times one can call on Green Tara with ease and obtain her assistance for compassionate acts. 300 multiplied by 700 is 210,000, for a total of 910,000 mantra repetitions. 910,000 divided by 84,000 equals 10.83333333333333, another fascinating result, that despite the decimal point, depicts 108 before the following neat sequence of threes. The practice has a series of esoteric design however the activating Green Tara mantra is commonly used on its own, Om Tare Tu Tare Ture Swa Ha.

109. Maintain a practice. The japa mala beads, so important to so many meditators, especially among Hindus, Buddhists and Sikhs, each a string of 108 beads all actually have a 109th bead. It's called the guru bead or summit stone and protrudes outward from the rest of the string. It is used to keep track of the number of mantra repetitions as one counts the number of revolutions through each time one's fingers come across the guru bead, 100 for each revolution, the extra 8 being for the guru, all sentient beings and/or covering errors. Traditionally one never crosses the guru bead, but goes back around the other way. Japa means quiet or inner utterance and mala is the string itself.

The repetition of mantras is meant to turn off the cycle of negative or mundane thinking, as a means of sense-withdrawal. Turning off mundane thinking leads to transcendent thinking toward enlightenment. Mantra chanting is one of many tools to turn off the five senses that constantly need to be fed with sensation, distracting the otherwise innate ability to seek, see, and gain enlightenment. To find our way to enlightenment we first must shut up the otherwise mundane inner utterances. The guru bead keeps our mind focused on the sound and meaning of the mantra, helping to prevent the wandering mind from losing focus on the sound and meaning rather than the run on sentence that our thinking can be. When one reaches the guru bead one stops and then revolves in the opposite direction symbolizing the solstices, and more deeply the connection of the macrocosm with the microcosm in turning the mala, the connection of the universe and the universal self. We are all strung together, all connected, this universal connection is within the individual, just as the string is within the bead.

Spiritually the sound of the mantra is important. Sanskrit is mathematically harmonious language, so the sounds correlate with macrocosmic with the microcosmic. However, the mind state is much more important than the sound one utters, than the pronunciation. The invocation is more important than the verbalization. As mechanical as some meditations and meditative movements may be the benefits are tangible and more so when the mind is right, even if the movement is off.

In order to be a good teacher, be a good student. It's said that one finds the right teacher in life only when one is ready. Do not worry so much about the quality of your teachers, or the teachers available to you, worry about the quality of yourself as a student. Even the most wretched angry drunks can teach quality lessons to a good student. In order to be a good teacher and a guru to others around you simply be good student yourself and eventually people will learn from you. To teach effectively one must practice with students, as well as offer clear instructions. To learn effectively one must practice on your own and pay attention.

Tai chi practitioners refer to this refinement through the lesson of inches. It applies to learning the long form, but also to life in general. First one mimics the movement to about a foot away from correct posture, then one refines it to within an inch difference between teacher and student, then a tenth of an inch and then to within the width of hair's difference. There is also the inches mistake in tai chi. This refers to the idea that one should be mindful of one's posture and other key elements before advancing or else a mistake of one inch even at a slow velocity can lead to be wildly off course if we stay steered in that direction.

To be a good teacher or guru, don't focus on mastership, focus on being a practitioner. When you're climbing you're a climber, not just on top or on bottom of the mountain, one should think the same way concerning any practice and life. Be a practitioner, instead of master or student, as one lives life and practices whatever. This development of self is a never ending climb, that is it can be. It ends when you decide it does. There is no finishing, just practice and refinement.

Please leave a review for 108 Steps to Be in The Zone on amazon.com. Reviews make all the digital difference for an indie author.

Please read Ethan Indigo Smith's other books like The Matrix of Four, The Geometry of Energy, Tibetan Fusion, The Little Green Book of Revolution, The Terraist Letters and The New Printed Threat.

Do you have a story about 108 or point of interest you'd like to share? Find Ethan Indigo Smith via simple internet search.

Made in the USA
Charleston, SC
19 May 2016